CONFUCIUS

The Great Digest
The Unwobbling Pivot
The Analects

Stone Text from
rubbings supplied by
WILLIAM HAWLEY

A Note on the
Stone Editions by
ACHILLES FANG

TRANSLATION & COMMENTARY BY

EZRA POUND

CONFUCIUS

THE GREAT DIGEST
THE UNWOBBLING PIVOT
THE ANALECTS

A NEW DIRECTIONS BOOK

CONTENTS

An Edition

for

Walter de Rachewiltz

A NOTE ON THE STONE-CLASSICS

and the books were incised in stone
46 tablets set up at the door of the college
— *Canto LIV* (*page* 27)

In order to establish a standard text of the corpus of Confucian classics, several Chinese dynasties had them incised on stone tablets, which were placed in the Imperial Academy in the metropolis. The editio princeps was produced in the latter days of the Han dynasty, between 175 and 183 A.D. But the stones had to go the way of all books:

And the 46 tablets that stood there in Lo Yang
were broken and built into Foé's temple (Foés,
that is goddam bhuddists.)
this was under Hou-chi the she empress.
— *Canto LIV* (*page* 30)

This refers to the year 518 A.D. At present some three hundred fragments of the 46 tablets are known to exist.

The immediately succeeding dynasty, Wei, set up its Stone-Classics sometime between 240 and 249 A.D. by the side of the Han stones at Lo-yang. The unique feature of the Wei stones is that they are inscribed with three styles of calligraphy. Of the original 35 stones a little over 140 fragments still exist.

Passing over the putative stones of the Chin and Toba-Wei dynasties, we come to the great T'ang dynasty. As the Chinese text printed in this book is derived from the T'ang stones, the second part of this note will discuss them in detail.

The short-lived dynasty of Shu (present Ssuch'uan) started its Stone-Classics in 938 A.D.; the work was completed by the Sung in 1124 A.D., long after that minor dynasty (capital: Ch'eng-tu) had perished. Unlike the preceding classics, the Shu classics comprised all the 13, for which more than a thousand stones were needed. Strangely, not a fragment is extant; there are, however, quite a number of their rubbings still available. Incidentally, it was about this time that the Confucian classics began to be printed from wood-blocks.

The Sung, in spite of internal dissensions and barbarian incursions, produced their Stone-Classics twice. It took them 19 years (1042-1061 A.D.) to bring out 9 classics at K'aifeng. It is not recorded how many stones were needed; only a few fragments are still extant. After they had moved their capital to present Hang-chou, they set up 6 classics and a portion of the Li-chi (Li-ki), including Chung-yung and Tahsio. The work took them more than a generation (1135-1177 A.D.). There still exist 86 stones; there is no means of determining the original number of the stones.

Finally, the emperor Ch'ien-lung of the Ch'ing (Manchu) dynasty set up, 1791-1794 A.D., 189 stones inscribed with the text of all the 13 classics. They are still preserved in Peking (see photo on jacket).

The Stone-Classics of the T'ang dynasty, from a rubbing of which the Chinese text of this book is derived, were begun in 833 A.D. and completed in 837; they originally comprised 12 classics, the missing 13th being the Book of Mencius, which had not then acquired the status of a Confucian classic. The text and apparatus criticus, 650,252 characters in all, took 227 stones, each measuring 6 feet in height and over 2 feet in width. Originally set up in the Imperial Academy in Ch'ang-an (present Hsi-an), these stones have weathered fairly well; except for a few stones which suffered damage in the earthquake of 1555, they are still preserved intact in Hsi-an.

When Chu Hsi lifted chapter 31 (Chung-yung) and 42 (Ta-hsio) out of the Li-ki to make a Confucian quartet (he himself called it Ssu-shu, 'Four Books') by joining them with the Analects of Confucius and the Book of Mencius, he rearranged the sequence of the Ta-hsio text. Mr. Pound's translation follows Chu Hsi's edition; the text had to be re-edited (a mere scissors-&-paste job). As for Chung-yung, no juggling was needed. There are some minor textual variations in both texts between the T'ang reading and the Chu Hsi reading; they are, however, so unimportant that no retouching was deemed necessary.

It should be noted that most of the given names of T'ang emperors preceding Wen-tsung, in whose reign the Stone-Classics were made, are written minus the last stroke; e.g. 民 for 民 , because 世民 was the given name of T'ai-tsung. The same applies to compound characters containing imperial names.

The preface to the Ch'ing Stone-Classics, written in 1794 by Ch'ien-lung (who lived 1711-1799 and reigned 1736-1795), runs as follows:

". . . It was Chiang Heng who wrote down the text of these classics; he offered his calligraphy to the throne in

13

1740. As there were some minor errors in it, I made the Academicians go through it. After which I had it stored in the high halls of Mou-ch'in-tien (in the palace) for the past fifty-odd years; meanwhile I forgot their existence. Some years ago, the editors of the second series of the Shih-ch'ü pao-chi catalogue called my attention to Chiang Heng's calligraphy, when I was delighted and said to myself: 'Indeed! indeed! This cannot be considered as an ordinary sort of calligraphy in which I may take pleasure in times of leisure. No, it must be engraved on stone and placed in the imperial academy, to serve as a memento for the future of how I revered learning and esteemed the process (*tao*). Classics are the norm, the process; and a norm never varies and the process is what is constant, for Heaven and the process never change. These words of Tung Chung-shu hit the mark.'

It was the Han who first set up their 'one-character' stones; then the Wei carried on the tradition with theirs written in three sorts of characters. Of these two, however, we lack detailed information. Stone-Classics were also made by the T'ang and the Sung, both Northern and Southern; they are either erroneous or incomplete . . . .

Old as I am, I am still avid of learning and never relent. I blush to think how little I know. But I must congratulate myself upon having set up these stones in the imperial academy; for they, a work done at the opportune moment, embody the tradition of the sages and stand as a norm for the future. They will serve as a guide for scholars. Chiang Heng's assiduity has now borne fruit.

As for the commentaries transmitted from the past dynasties, they have now usurped the place of the text itself. There is so much controversy and polemic over them; moreover, they are so profuse and prolix. It was, therefore, quite right of Chiang Heng to write down the text only. Some may object to this, alleging that the text cannot be understood without the commentary. My answer is that it would be far better to let the text explain itself than to explain it by means of the commentary. If a student concentrates and uses his mind, he will discover the process (*tao*) between the lines. If he compares the text of the six classics with each other, he will be able to get to the fons et origo and unravel the mystery. It all depends on his labor and intelligence. Moreover, the 13 classics with running commentary that I had reprinted from wood-blocks are still abundantly available."

—*Achilles Fang*

TÁ HSIO
THE GREAT DIGEST

NOTE

Starting at the bottom as market inspector, having risen to be Prime Minister, Confucius is more concerned with the necessities of government, and of governmental administration than any other philosopher. He had two thousand years of documented history behind him which he condensed so as to render it useful to men in high official position, not making a mere collection of anecdotes as did Herodotus.

His analysis of why the earlier great emperors had been able to govern greatly was so sound that every durable dynasty, since his time, has risen on a Confucian design and been initiated by a group of Confucians. China was tranquil when her rulers understood these few pages. When the principles here defined were neglected, dynasties waned and chaos ensued. The proponents of a world order will neglect at their peril the study of the only process that has repeatedly proved its efficiency as social coordinate.

TERMINOLOGY

示   The light descending (from the sun, moon and stars.) To be watched as component in ideograms indicating spirits, rites, ceremonies.

明   The sun and moon, the total light process, the radiation, reception and reflection of light; hence, the intelligence. Bright, brightness, shining. Refer to Scotus Erigena, Grosseteste and the notes on light in my *Cavalcanti*.

誠   "Sincerity." The precise definition of the word, pictorially the sun's lance coming to rest on the precise spot verbally. The righthand half of this compound means: to perfect, bring to focus.

The eye (at the right) looking straight into the heart.

What results, i.e., the action resultant from this straight gaze into the heart. The "know thyself" carried into action. Said action also serving to clarify the self knowledge. To translate this simply as "virtue" is on a par with translating rhinoceros, fox and giraffe indifferently by "quadruped" or "animal."

The man in two successive positions. Serves as prefix to indicate motion or action.

The will, the direction of the will, *directio voluntatis*, the officer standing over the heart.

志

To succeed in due hour. Prefix action taking effect at the sun's turn.

得

Fidelity to the given word. The man here standing by his word.

信

Humanitas, humanity, in the full sense of the word, "manhood." The man and his full contents.

The process. Footprints and the foot carrying the head; the head conducting the feet, an orderly movement under lead of the intelligence.

保佑命

This phrase—nourishing, supporting the destiny—should be compared with the *Odyssey*, I, 34.

This ideogram for a spirit contains two elements to be watched.

One readily sees the similarity of this element to the bent heraldic arm of Armstrong and Strongi'tharm. I have never found it in composition save where there is indication of energy, I think we may say, a source of personally directed energy.

儿

The running legs indicate rapid motion or at least the capacity for motion.

THE STONE-CLASSICS title refers to the Nineteenth Roll of the book of *CEREMONIES*, and divides the Great Learning into 42 sections. Notes from E.P.'s earlier edition are left where they were.

CHU HSI'S PREFACE

My master the Philosopher Ch'eng says: The Great
Learning, Great Digest, is the testament of Confucius,
transmitted, the initial study for whomso would pass
the gate into virtue. If we today can see how the men
of old went about their study, it is due solely to the con-
servation of these strips of bamboo; the Analects and
the Book of Mencius are subsequent.

He who studies must start from this meridian and
study with warm precision; cutting to this homely
pattern he will not botch.

禮記卷第十九

大學第四十二　鄭氏注

大學之道在明明德在親

CONFUCIUS' TEXT

1.

 The great learning [adult study, grinding the corn in the head's mortar to fit it for use] takes root in clarifying the way wherein the intelligence increases through the process of looking straight into one's own heart and acting on the results; it is rooted in watching with affection the way people grow;

已在止於至善知止而后
有定定而后能靜靜而后
能安安而后能慮慮而后
能得物有本末事有終始
知所先後則近道矣古之
欲明明德於天下者先治

it is rooted in coming to rest, being at ease in perfect equity.

2.

    Know the point of rest and then have an orderly mode of procedure; having this orderly procedure one can "grasp the azure," that is, take hold of a clear concept; holding a clear concept one can be at peace [internally], being thus calm one can keep one's head in moments of danger; he who can keep his head in the presence of a tiger is qualified to come to his deed in due hour.

3.

    Things have roots and branches; affairs have scopes and beginnings. To know what precedes and what follows, is nearly as good as having a head and feet.

    Mencius' epistemology starts from this verse.

4.

    The men of old wanting to clarify and diffuse throughout the empire that light which comes from looking straight into the heart and then acting, first set up good government

其國欲治其國者先齊其
家欲齊其家者先脩其
欲脩其身者先正其心
正其心者先誠其意欲
其意者先致其知致知在
格物物格而后知至知至

in their own states; wanting good government in their states, they first established order in their own families; wanting order in the home, they first disciplined themselves; desiring self-discipline, they rectified their own hearts; and
wanting to rectify their hearts, they
sought precise verbal definitions of their
inarticulate thoughts [the tones given
off by the heart]; wishing to attain precise verbal definitions, they set to extend
their knowledge to the utmost. This completion of knowledge is rooted in sorting
things into organic categories.

5.
     When things had been classified in
organic categories, knowledge moved
toward fulfillment; given the extreme
knowable points,

而后意誠意誠而后心正

心正而后身脩身脩而后

家齊家齊家齊而后國治國治

而后天下平自天子以至

於庶人壹是皆以脩身為

本其本亂而末治者否矣

the inarticulate thoughts were defined with precision [the sun's lance coming to rest on the precise spot verbally]. Having attained this precise verbal definition [*aliter*, this sincerity], they then stabilized their hearts, they disciplined themselves; having attained self-discipline, they set their own houses in order; having order in their own homes, they brought good government to their own states; and when their states were well governed, the empire was brought into equilibrium.

6.

From the Emperor, Son of Heaven, down to the common man, singly and all together, this self-discipline is the root.

7.

If the root be in confusion, nothing will be well governed.

其所厚者薄而其所薄者

厚未之有也康誥曰克明

德大甲曰顧諟天之明命

帝典曰克明峻德皆自明

也湯之盤銘曰苟日新日

日新又曰新康誥曰作新

The solid cannot be swept away as trivial, nor can trash be established as solid. It just doesn't happen.

"Take not cliff for morass and treacherous bramble."

The preceding is the first chapter of the canon containing Confucius' words as Tseng Tsze has handed them down. Now follow ten chapters of Tseng's thoughts as his disciples recorded them. In the oldest copies there was a certain confusion due to the shuffling of the original bamboo tablets. Now, basing myself on Ch'eng's conclusions, and having reexamined the classic text, I have arranged them as follows. ("On the left," in the Chinese method of writing.) —Chu Hsi.

明

TSENG'S COMMENT

I

1.

It is said in the K'ang Proclamation: He showed his intelligence by acting straight from the heart.

2.

It is said in the Great Announcement: He contemplated the luminous decree of heaven, and found the precise word wherewith to define it.

3.

It is said in the Canon of the Emperor (Yau): His intelligence shone vital over the hill-crest, he clarified the high-reaching virtue, *id est*, that action which is due to direct self-knowledge.

4.

All these statements proceed from the ideogram of the sun and moon standing together [that is, from the ideogram which expresses the total light process].

明

This is the first chapter of the comment giving the gist (sorting out the grist) of the expressions: Make clear the intelligence by looking straight into the heart and then acting. Clarify the intelligence in straight action.

II

1.

In letters of gold on T'ang's bath-tub:

日
日
新

As the sun makes it new
Day by day make it new
Yet again make it new.

2.

It is said in the K'ang Proclamation: *He is risen, renewing the people.*

3.

The *Odes* say:

Although Chou was an ancient kingdom
The celestial destiny
Came again down on it NEW.

—*Shi King*, III, 1, 1, 1.
(*Decade of King Wen*)

Tseng's
Comment

已詩曰周雖舊邦其命惟

新是故君子無所不用其

極詩云邦畿千里維民所

止詩云緡蠻黃鳥止于丘

隅子曰於止知其所止可

以人而不如鳥乎詩云穆

4.

Hence the man in whom speaks the voice of his forebears cuts no log that he does not make fit to be roof-tree [does nothing that he does not bring to a maximum, that he does not carry through to a finish].

This is the second chapter of the comment containing and getting the grist of the phrase: Renew the people.
Ideogram: axe, tree and wood-pile.

新

III

1.

The *Book of Poems* says:
The royal domain is of 1000 li
Thither the people would fly to its rest
  [would hew out its resting place].

    —*Shi King*, IV, 3, 3, 4.

2.

The *Book of Poems* says:
The twittering yellow bird,
The bright silky warbler
Talkative as a cricket
Comes to rest in the hollow corner
  of the hill.

    —*Shi King*, II, 8, 6, 2.

Kung said: comes to its rest, alights, knows what its rest is, what its ease is. Is man, for all his wit, less wise than this bird of the yellow plumage that he should not know his resting place or fix the point of his aim?

39

穆文王於緝熙敬止為人

君止於仁為人臣止於敬

為人子止於孝為人父止

於慈與國人交止於信詩

云瞻彼淇澳菉竹猗猗有

斐君子如切如磋如琢如

3.
The *Odes* say:

As a field of grain
White-topped in even order,
The little flowing ears of grain
Bending in white, even order,
So glorious was King Wan,
Coherent, splendid and reverent
In his comings to rest, in his bournes.

    —Shi King, III, 1, 1, 4.

As prince he came to rest in humanity, in
the full human qualities, in his manhood;
As a minister, in respect;
As a son, in filial devotion;
As a father in carrying kindliness down
into particular acts, and in relation to the
people, in fidelity to his given word.

4.
The *Odes* say:

Cast your eye on Ch'i river,
The slow water winding
Bright reflecting the shaggy bamboo;
Shaggy green are the flowing leaves,
Shaggy the bamboo above it,
Our Lord has so many talents
As we cut,
As we file,
As we carve the jade and grind it,

磨瑟兮僩兮赫兮喧兮有
斐君子終不可諠兮如切
如磋者道學也如琢如磨
者自脩也瑟兮僩兮者恂
慄也赫兮喧兮者威儀也
有斐君子終不可諠兮者

Firm in decision, Oh!
On guard against calumny
                    and its makers, oh!
Splendid, oh! oh!
His voice our impulse, Aye!
A prince of many talents, who will
                    carry through to the end,
Who will not go back on his word.

                    —*Shi King*, I, 5, 1, 1.

"As we cut, as we file," refers to the intelligent method of study; "As we carve
the jade and grind it" refers to the self-
discipline; "Firm in decision, on guard
against calumny and its makers" indicates his anxiety to be fair; "Splendid,
his voice our impulse" indicates his stern
equity in the halls of judgment; "A
prince of many talents, who will carry
through to the end, who will not go back
on his word" indicates that style of conduct offered as the

道盛德至善民之不能忘
也詩云於戲前王不忘君
子賢其賢而親其親小人
樂其樂而利其利此以沒
世不忘也子曰聽訟吾猶
人也必也使無訟乎無情

grain to the gods, without blemish, total in rectitude, and this the people cannot forget.

5.

The *Odes* say:
In our ceremonial plays,
In the ritual dances
        with tiger masks and spears
The archetype kings are not forgotten.
                —*Shi King*, IV, 1, 4, 3.

The great gentlemen honor the worth they honored and hold in attentive affection the growing and ordered things which they held in affection; the lesser folk delight in that wherein the ancient kings delighted and profit by what profited them [their canals and good customs]; thus the generations pass like water and the former kings are not forgotten.

> *This is the third chapter of the comment sifting out the grist of the phrase: be at ease in total rectitude.*
>
> *Whether the ideogram indicating distinctions, which Legge translates "former," starts out by indicating a cutting of meat after hunting or a measuring of the different slices of the moon astronomically, I cannot say, nor do I remember whether Karlgren has an opinion on it.*

IV

Kung said: In hearing law-suits I am no worse than anyone else, but one should eliminate law-suits. If the not quite candid were

止於至善

45

者不得盡其辭大畏民志
此謂知本此謂知本此謂
知之至也所謂誠其意者
毋自欺也如惡惡臭如好
好色此之謂自謙故君子
必慎其獨也小人閒居為

unable to pour out their rhetoric to the full, a greater awe and respect [for government justice] would prevail in the popular mind. This is called knowing the root.

> *This is the fourth chapter of the comment giving the gist of the remark (in the Confucian canon) about the root and the branch.*

V

This is called knowing the root.
This is called completing the cognitions.

> *There is here a lacuna in place of the fifth chapter of the comment. Ch'eng's speculation about it was not essential to E. P.'s earlier edition and is not in the Stone-Classics as the reader can see for himself.*

VI

1.

Finding the precise word for the inarticulate heart's tone means not lying to oneself, as in the case of hating a bad smell or loving a beautiful person, also called respecting one's own nose.

On this account the real man has to look his heart in the eye even when he is alone.

2.

There is, for the small man living unobserved,

不善無所不至見君子而

后厭然揜其不善而著其

善人之視己如見其肺肝

然則何益矣此謂誠於中

形於外故君子必慎其獨

也曾子曰十目所視十手

no iniquity that he will not carry through to the limit; if he sees a true man he turns and takes cover, hides his iniquities, sticks out his merits, but the other fellow sees the significance of this as if he saw into his lungs and liver; what is the good of his faking, what dish does it cover?

That is the meaning of the saying: the true word is in the middle inside and will show on the outside. Therefore the man of real breeding who carries the cultural and moral heritage must look his heart in the eye when alone.

3.

Tseng Tsze said: what ten eyes gaze at, what ten hands

所指其嚴乎富潤屋德潤

身心廣體胖故君子必誠

其意所謂脩身在正其心

者身有所忿懥則不得其

正有所恐懼則不得其正

有所好樂則不得其正有

point to should preserve a certain decorum [ought to be mentionable, discussable].

4.

You improve the old homestead by material riches and irrigation; you enrich and irrigate the character by the process of looking straight into the heart and then acting on the results. Thus the mind becomes your palace and the body can be at ease; it is for this reason that the great gentleman must find the precise verbal expression for his inarticulate thoughts.

This is the sixth chapter of the comment, sorting out the grist of the sentence about finding precise verbal expression for the heart's tone, for the inarticulate thoughts.

The dominant ideograms in the chapter are the sun's lance falling true on the word, and the heart giving off tone.

VII

1.

In the phrase, "Self discipline is rooted in rectification of the heart," the word rectify (*cheng*) can be illustrated as follows: if there be a knife of resentment in the heart or enduring rancor, the mind will not attain precision; under suspicion and fear it will not form sound judgment, nor will it, dazzled by love's delight

51

所憂患則不得其正心不
在焉視而不見聽而不聞
食而不知其味此謂脩身
在正其心所謂齊其家在
脩其身者人之其所親愛
而辟焉之其所賤惡而辟

nor in sorrow and anxiety, come to precisions.

2.

If the heart have not stable root, eager for justice, one looks and sees not [looks and sees phantoms]; listens and hears not [listens internally and does not hear objectively]; eats and knows not the flavors.

That is what we mean by saying: self-discipline is rooted in rectifying the heart.

This is the seventh chapter of the commentary giving the gist of: "rectifying the heart disciplines the character."

As to the frequent lack of tense indications, the ideogramic mind assumes that what has been, is and will be. Only the exception, or the sequence of events requires further indications. See also verse 3 of the canon.

VIII

I.

The phrase, "Regulation of the family is rooted in self-discipline," can be understood by observing that men love what they see growing up under their own roof, and show partiality; if they have something in contempt and hate it, they are partial;

焉之其所畏敬而辟
其所哀矜而辟焉之
敖惰而辟焉故好而知其
惡惡而知其美者天下鮮
矣故諺有之曰人莫知其
子之惡莫知其苗之碩此

if they are filled with reverence and respect, they are partial; if they feel sorrow
and compassion, they are partial; and
then someone comes arrogantly along
paying no attention to us, and our judgment of them is thereby influenced.
There are, thus, few men under heaven
who can love and see the defects, or hate
and see the excellence of an object.

*Tseng's
Comment*

2.

   Hence the shaggy proverb: No man
knows his son's faults, no one knows
the stone-hard grain in the stalk's head
from the first sprouts.

謂身不脩不可以齊其家

所謂治國必先齊其家者

其家不可教而能教人者

無之故君子不出家而成

教於國孝者所以事君也

弟者所以事長也慈者所

3.

That is the meaning of the saying: If a man does not discipline himself he cannot bring order into the home.

*This is the eighth chapter of the comment
dealing with self-discipline and domestic
order.*

IX

1.

What is meant by saying, "To govern a state one must first bring order into one's family," is this: the man who,
being incapable of educating his own
family, is able to educate other men just
doesn't exist. On which account the real
man perfects the nation's culture without leaving his fireside. There, at home,
is the filial sense whereby a prince is ser-
ved; there the fraternal deference that
serves in relations to one's elders and to
those in higher grade; there the kindness in matters of detail that is needed

以使眾也康誥曰如保赤
子心誠求之雖不中不
遠矣未有學養子而后嫁
者也一家仁一國興仁一
家讓一國興讓一人貪戾
一國作亂其機如此此謂

in dealing with the mass of people.

2.

The K'ang Proclamation says: "As if taking care of an infant." If the heart sincerely wants to, although one may not hit the mark precisely in the center, one won't go far wrong. No girl ever yet studied suckling a baby in order to get married.

3.

One humane family can humanize a whole state; one courteous family can lift a whole state into courtesy; one grasping and perverse man can drive a nation to chaos. Such are the seeds of movement [*semina motuum*, the inner impulses of the tree]. That is what we mean by:

一言僨事一人定國堯舜
率天下以仁而已從之桀
紂率天下以暴而已從之
其所令反其所好而已不
從是故君子有諸己而后
求諸人無諸己而后非諸

one word will ruin the business, one man
can bring the state to an orderly course.

4.

Yau and Shun led the empire by
their humanity and the people followed;
Chieh and Chou governed the empire
with overweening violence and the people
copied their conduct, their imperial orders being in contradiction to their likes,
the people did not follow the orders.

Whence we note that the prince must
have in himself not one but all of the
qualities that he requires from others,
and must himself be empty of what he
does not want from others in reflex.

人所藏乎身不恕而能喻
諸人者未之有也故治國
在齊其家詩云桃之夭夭
其葉蓁蓁之子于歸宜
其家人宜其家人而后可
以教國人詩云宜兄宜弟

No one has ever yet been able to induct others into a style of conduct not part of his own viscera.

5.

That is why the government of a state is rooted in keeping order in one's own family.

6.

The *Odes* say:

Delicate as the peach-tree in blossom
The leaves abundant as grass-blades,
Fragile fair she goes
>   *to the house of her husband,*
The bride who will bring harmony to it
As an altar raised on earth
>   *under heaven.*

>   —*Shi King*, I, 1, 6, 3.

As an altar bringing harmony and order into the home. Given that, one can teach the people throughout the state.

7.

The *Odes* say:

In harmony with heaven above
And with earth below
The elder and younger brothers
About an altar, in harmony.

>   —*Shi King*, II, 2, 9, 3.

When there is this harmony between elder and younger brothers you can educate the men of the nation.

63

宜兄宜弟而后可以教國
人詩云其儀不忒正是四
國其為父子兄弟足法而
后民法之也此謂治國在
齊其家所謂平天下在治
其國者上老老而民興孝

8.

The *Odes* say:

He practiced equity without
its making him feel
That a javelin were being
thrust into his heart.

—*Shi King*, I, 14, 3, 3.

[*Aliter*, faultlessly.] On these lines he rectified the state to its four angles. When right conduct between father and son, between brother and younger brother, has become sufficiently instinctive, the people will follow the course as ruled.

9.

That is the meaning of: The government of the state is rooted in family order.

This is the ninth chapter of the comment giving the gist of: Put order in the home in order to govern the country.

X

1.

The meaning of, "World Order [bringing what is under heaven into equilibrium] is rooted in the good government of one's own state," is this: If those in high place respect the aged, the people will bring filial piety to a high level;

上長長而民興弟上恤孤
而民不倍是以君子有絜
矩之道也所惡於上毋以
下所惡於下毋以事上所
惡於前毋以先後所惡於
後毋以從前所惡於右毋

if those in high place show deference to their elders, the people will bring their fraternal deference to a high level; if those in high place pity orphans, the people will not do otherwise; it is by this that the great gentlemen have a guide to conduct, a compass and square of the process.

2.

If you hate something in your superiors, do not practice it on those below you; if you hate a thing in those below you, do not do it when working for those over you. If you hate something in the man ahead of you, do not do it to the fellow who follows you; if a thing annoy you from the man at your heels, do not push it at the man in front of you.

以交於左所惡於左母以
交於右此之謂絜矩之道
詩云樂只君子民之父母
民之所好好之民之所惡
惡之此之謂民之父母詩
云節彼南山維石巖巖赫

Do not in your relations with your left-hand neighbor what annoys you if done at your right, nor in your relations to your right-hand neighbor what annoys you if done at your left. This is called having a compass and T-square of the process.

3.

The *Odes* say:

What a joy are these princes
At once father and mother
of their people.
—*Shi King*, II, 2, 5, 3.

To love what the people love and hate what is bad for the people [what they hate] is called being the people's father and mother.

4.

The *Odes* say:

South Mountain
Cutting the horizon, fold over fold,
Steep cliffs full of voices and echoes,
Towering over the echoes,
Towering;

赫師尹巳具爾瞻有國者
不可以不慎辟則爲天下
僇矣詩云殷之未喪師克
配上帝儀監于殷峻命不
易道得眾則得國失眾則
失國是故君子先慎乎德

Resplendent, resplendent,
>*Yin, Lord Conductor,*
The people gaze at you,
>*muttering under their breath.*
>>*—Shi King, II, 4, 7, 1.*
(Chia-fu's invective against Yin)

Those who have rule over states and families cannot but look themselves straight in the heart; if they deviate they bring shame on the whole empire.

5.

The *Odes* say:

Until the Yin had lost the assembly . . .
They could offer the cup and drink with
The Most Highest.

>*—Shi King, III, 1, 1, 6.*

We can measure our regard for equity by the Yin. High destiny is not easy. Right action gains the people* and that gives one the state. Lose the people, you lose the state.

6.

Therefore the great gentleman starts by looking straight into his heart to see how he is getting on with the process of acting

---

* I think this ideogram has an original sense of the people gathered at its tribal blood rite.

有德此有人此有人此有土

有土此有財有財此有用

德者本也財者末也外本

內末爭民施奪是故財聚

則民散財散則民聚是故

言悖而出者亦悖而入貨

on the basis of such direct observation.
When he can see and act straight in this,
he will have the people with him; having the people, he will have the territory;
having the land, the product will be under his control, and controling this wealth
he will have the means to act and make
use of it.

7.

The *virtu*, i.e., this self-knowledge
[looking straight into the heart and acting thence] is the root; the wealth is a
by-product.

8.

If you leave the root in the open and
plant the branch, you will merely em-
broil the people and lead them to robbing
hen-roosts.

9.

Rake in wealth and you scatter the
people. Divide the wealth and the people will gather to you.

10.

Words that go out a-wry, pettishly,
will return as turmoil,

73

悖而入者亦悖而出康誥
曰惟命不于常道善則得
之不善則失之矣楚書曰
楚國無以為寶惟善以為
寶舅犯曰亡人無以為寶
仁親以為寶秦誓曰若有

and as for money: ill got, ill go.

11.

The K'ang Proclamation has said:
Heaven's decree is not given in perman-
ence: Proceeding with rightness you attain it, and with unrightness spew it
away.

12.

In the Ch'u History it is said: The
Ch'u state does not go in for collecting
wealth [treasuring porcelain, jewels and
money] but counts fair-dealing* its treasure.

13.

Uncle Fan (refusing an offer of
bribery) said: The lost man [King Wen
in exile] does not treasure jewels and
such wealth, counting his manhood and
the love of his relatives the true treasure.

14.

It is said in the Ch'in Declaration:
If I had

---

* Legge says "its good men."

75

一介臣斷斷兮無他技其
心休休焉其如有容焉人
之有技若己有之人之彥
聖其心好之不啻若自其
口出寔能容之以能保我
子孫黎民尚亦有利哉人

but one straight minister who could cut
the cackle [ideogram of the ax and the
documents of the archives tied up in
silk], yes, if without other abilities save
simple honesty, a moderate spender but
having the magnanimity to recognize
talent in others, it would be as if he himself had those talents; and when others
had erudition and wisdom he would
really like it and love them, not merely
talk about it and make a show from the
mouth outward but solidly respect them,
and be able to stand having talented men
about him; such a man could sustain my
sons and descendents and the black-
haired people, and benefits would mount
up from him.

之有技媚疾以惡之人之
彥聖而違之俾不通寔不
能容以不能保我子孫黎
巳亦曰殆哉唯仁人放流
之逬諸四夷不與同中國
此謂唯仁人爲能愛人能

But if, when others have ability, he acts like a jealous female sick with envy, and hates them; and if, when others have knowledge and sage judgment, he shoves them out of the way and prevents their promotion and just can't stand 'em when they have real worth, he will *not* preserve my sons and grandsons and the Chinese people, in fact he can be called a real pest.

15.

Only the fully humane man will throw out such a minister and send him off among the barbarians of the frontiers. He will not associate with him in the Middle Kingdom; that is what is meant by: Only the fully humane man can love another; or can

惡人見賢而不能舉舉而
不能先命也見不善而不
能退退而不能遠過也好
人之所惡惡人之所好是
謂拂人之性菑必逮夫身
是故君子有大道必忠信

really hate him.

16.

To see high merit and be unable to raise it to office, to raise it but not to give such promotion precedence, is just destiny; to see iniquity and not have the capacity to throw it out; to throw it out and not have the capacity to send it to distant exile, is to err.

17.

To love what the people hate, to hate what they love is called doing violence to man's inborn nature. Calamities will come to him who does this [definite physical calamities], the wild grass will grow over his dead body.

18.

Thus the true man has his great mode of action which must be from the plumb center of his heart, maintaining his given word

以得之驕泰以失之生財
有大道生之者眾食之者
寡為之者疾用之者舒則
財恆足矣仁者以財發身
不仁者以身發財未有上
好仁而下不好義者也未

that he come to his deed in due hour.
Pride and jactancy lose all this.

19.

And there is a chief way for the
production of wealth, namely, that the
producers be many and that the mere
consumers be few; that the artisan mass
be energetic and the consumers temper-
ate, then the constantly circulating goods
will be always a-plenty.*

20.

"Good king is known by his spend-
ing, ill lord by his taking." The humane
man uses his wealth as a means to distinction, the inhumane becomes a mere
harness, an accessory to his takings.

21.

There has never been in high place
a lover of the human qualities, of full
manhood, but that those below him loved
equity.

---

* I think the ideogram indicates not only a constant
 circulation of goods but also a sort of alluvial
 deposit all along the course of the circuit.

有好義其事不終者也未
有府庫財非其財者也
孟獻子曰畜馬乘不察於
雞豚伐冰之家不畜牛羊
百乘之家不畜聚斂之臣
與其有聚斂之臣寧有盜

Never have such lovers of equity failed to carry through their work to completion, nor have the treasures in such a ruler's libraries and arsenals not been used to his benefit and stayed his.

22.

The official, Meng Hsien, said: Men who keep horses and carriages do not tend fowls and pigs; a family that uses ice in its ancestral ceremonies does not run a cattle and sheep farm; one having a fief of a hundred war chariots does not maintain a minister to clap people into the Black Maria [for non-payment of unjust taxes]. Rather than have a minister who claps people into the police van [nefariously] it would be better to have one who robs the state funds.

臣此謂國不以利為利以
義為利也長國家而務財
用者必自小人矣彼為善
之小人之使為國家菑害
並至雖有善者亦無如之
何矣此謂國不以利為利

That is the significance of the phrase: a country does not profit by making profits, its equity is its profit.

23.
When the head of a state or family thinks first of gouging out an income, he must perforce do it through small men; and even if they are clever at their job, if one employ such inferior characters in state and family business the tilled fields will go to rack swamp and ruin and edged calamities will mount up to the full; and even if, thereafter, an honest man be brought into the administration he will not be then able to find remedy for these ills.

That is the meaning of:
A state does not profit by profits.

以義為利也

禮記卷第十九

Honesty is the treasure of states.

The old commentator ends by saying: "Despise not this comment because of its simplicity."

The translator would end by asking the reader to keep on re-reading the whole digest until he understands HOW these few pages contain the basis on which the great dynasties were founded and endured, and why, lacking this foundation, the other and lesser dynasties perished quickly.

D.T.C., Pisa;
5 October—5 November, 1945.

"We are at the crisis point
of the world."

—Tami Kume, 1924.

利以義爲利也　　　"Equity is the Treasure of States"　　　國不以利爲

CHUNG YUNG
THE UNWOBBLING
PIVOT

NOTE

The second of the Four Classics, Chung Yung, *THE UNWOBBLING PIVOT*, contains what is usually supposed not to exist, namely the Confucian metaphysics. It is divided into three parts: the axis; the process; and sincerity, the perfect word, or the precise word; into

Metaphysics:

Only the most absolute sincerity under heaven can effect any change.

Politics:

In cutting an axe-handle the model is not far off, in this sense: one holds one axe-handle while chopping the other. Thus one uses men in governing men.

Ethics:

The archer, when he misses the bullseye, turns and seeks the cause of the error in himself.

CHU HSI'S PREFACE

My master the philosopher Ch'eng says: The word *chung* signifies what is bent neither to one side nor to the other. The word *yung* signifies unchanging. What exists plumb in the middle is the just process of the universe and that which never wavers or wobbles is the calm principle operant in its mode of action.

The spirit of this work comes from the door of Confucius, the heart's law transmitted *viva voce* from master to pupil, memorized and talked back and forth as mutual control of the invariable modus of action. Tsze Sze, fearing that with the passage of time the tradition might be distorted, wrote it out on the bamboo tablets and thus it came down to Mencius.

At its start the book speaks of the one principle, it then spreads into a discussion of things in general, and concludes by uniting all this in the one principle. Spread it out and its arrows reach to the six ends of the universe, zenith and nadir; fold it again and it withdraws to serve you in secret as faithful minister. Its savour is inexhaustible. It is, all of it, solid wisdom. The fortunate and attentive reader directing his mind to the solid, delighting in it as in a gem always carried, penetrating into its mysterious purity, when he has come to meridian, to the precise understanding, can use it till the end of his life, never exhausting it, never able to wear it out.

禮記卷第十六

中庸第卅一　　禮記

天命之謂性率性之謂道　　鄭氏注

循道之謂教道也者不可

PART ONE

TSZE SZE'S FIRST THESIS

I

1.

What heaven has disposed and sealed is called the inborn nature. The realization of this nature is called the process. The clarification of this process [the understanding or making intelligible of this process] is called education.

Note by Chu Hsi, an eleventh century commentator: The preceding is the first chapter in which Tsze Sze presents the tradition of the thought as the basis of his discourse. The main thing is to illumine the root of the process, a fountain of clear water descending from heaven immutable. The components, the bones of things, the materials are implicit and prepared in us, abundant and inseparable from us.*

Tsze Sze then speaks of the necessity of watching, nourishing, examining and re-examining them seriously and concludes by speaking of the way in which the spiritual nature of the sage carries his transmuting and operant power

(*Continued on page* 95)

* Cf. Shi King, III, 3, 6, 7.

須臾離也可離非道也是
故君子戒慎乎其所不睹
恐懼乎其所不聞莫見乎
隱莫顯乎微故君子慎其
獨也喜怒哀樂之未發謂
之中發而皆中節謂之和

2.

You do not depart from the process even for an instant; what you depart from is not the process. Hence the man who keeps rein on himself looks straight into his own heart at the things wherewith there is no trifling; he attends seriously to things unheard.

3.

Nothing is more outwardly visible than the secrets of the heart, nothing more obvious than what one attempts to conceal. Hence the man of true breed looks straight into his heart even when he is alone.

4.

Happiness, rage, grief, delight. To be unmoved by these emotions is to stand in the axis, in the center; being moved by these passions each in due degree constitutes being in harmony.

(*Note by Chu Hsi continued from page* 93)

to its utmost; his work to effect changes (land improvements, bettering of seed for example); all this stretching to an efficient life. The author wants the student to seek not a surface or single stratum of himself but to find his plumb center making use of himself.

Thus he would abandon every clandestine egoism and letch toward things extraneous to the real man in order to realize to the full the true root.

中也者天下之大本也和

也者天下之達道也致中

和天地位焉萬物育焉仲

尼曰君子中庸小人反中

庸君子之中庸也君子而

時中小人之中庸也小人

That axis in the center is the great root of the universe; that harmony is the universe's outspread process [of existence]. From this root and in this harmony, heaven and earth are established in their precise modalities, and the multitudes of all creatures persist, nourished on their meridians.

Yang Shih calls this chapter the essential marrow, the true meridian of the work. In the ten following chapters Tsze Sze cites certain phrases of Confucius in order to bring out the full sense of this initial statement.

II

1.

Chung Ni (Confucius) said: The master man finds the center and does not waver; the mean man runs counter to the circulation about the invariable.

The two ideograms chung *and* yung *represent most definitely a process in motion, an axis round which something turns.*

2.

The master man's axis does not wobble. The man of true breed finds this center in season, the small man's center is rigid, he pays no attention to the times and seasons, precisely because

而無忌憚也子曰中庸其
至矣乎民鮮能久矣子曰
道之不行也我知之矣知
者過之愚者不及也道之
不明也我知之矣賢者過
之不肖者不及也人莫不

he is a small man and lacking all reverence.

III

He said: Center oneself in the invariable: some have managed to do this, they
have hit the true center, and then?
Very few have been able to stay there.

IV

1.
    Kung said: People do not move in the
process. And I know why.
Those who know, exceed. (The intel-
ligentzia goes to extremes). The monkey-
minds don't get started. The process is
not understood. The men of talent shoot
past it, and the others do not get to it.

飲食也鮮能知味也子曰
道其不行矣夫子曰舜其
大知也與舜好問而好察
邇言隱惡而揚善執其兩
端用其中於民其斯以為
舜乎子曰人皆曰予知驅

2.

Everyone eats and drinks. Few can distinguish the flavors.

V

The Philosopher said: They do not proceed according to the process. No, people do not use the main open road.

VI

Kung said: Shun, for example, understood; he was a great and uprising knower. He liked to ask questions of people, and to listen to their simple answers. He passed over the malice and winnowed out the good. He observed their discordant motives and followed the middle line between these inharmonic extremes in governing the people, thus he deserved his name. [That is the significance of the ideogram "Shun" the hand which grasps, the cover that shields the discordant extremes.]

Further examination of the 136th radical might find a root for "the discordant opposites," in the signs of the waning and new-horned moon.

VII

Kung said: All men say: "Yes, I know." And in their excitement

而納諸罟擭陷阱之中而
莫之知辟也人皆曰予知
擇乎中庸而不能期月守
也子曰回之為人也擇乎
中庸得一善則拳拳服膺
而弗失之矣子曰天下國

they run wildly into every net and snare, falling plumb bang into the trap and none knows how to extricate himself therefrom. Everyone says: "Yes, we know." But if they manage to lay hold of the unwavering axis they can not keep a grip on it for a month.

VIII

Kung said: Hui's mode of action was to seize the unwavering axis, coming to an exact equity; he gripped it in his fist, and at once started using it, careful as if he were watching his chicken-coop, and he never let go or lost sight of it.

IX

Kung said: The empire, kingdoms,

家可均也爵祿可辭也白
刃可蹈也中庸不可能也
子路問強子曰南方之強
與北方之強與抑而強與
寬柔以教不報無道南方
之強也君子居之衽金革

families can be governed harmoniously; honors and salaries can be refused, you can tread sharp weapons and bright steel underfoot, without being able to stand firm in the unwavering center.

X

TSZE LU'S QUESTION

1.

Tsze Lu asked about energy.

2.

Kung answered: Do you mean the energy of the South or do you mean Nordic energy, or your own, that which you ought to have yourself and improve?

3.

To teach with kindly benevolence, not to lose one's temper and avenge the unreasonableness of others, that is the energy of the South. The wellbred man accumulates that sort of energy.

4.

To sleep on a heap of arms and untanned skins,

死而不厭北方之強也而

強者居之故君子和而不

流強哉矯中立而不倚強

哉矯國有道不變塞焉強

哉矯國無道至死不變強

哉矯子曰素隱行怪後世

to die unflinching and as if dying were not enough, that is Nordic energy and the energetic accumulate that sort of energy.

5.

Considering which things, the man of breed, in whom speaks the voice of his forebears, harmonizes these energies with no loss of his own direction; he stands firm in the middle of what whirls without leaning on anything either to one side or the other, his energy is admirably rectificative; if the country be well governed, he does not alter his way of life from what it had been during the establishment of the regime; when the country is ill governed, he holds firm to the end, even to death, unchanging. His is an admirably rectificative energy.

XI

1.

To seek mysteries in the obscure, poking into magic and committing eccentricities in order to be talked about later;

有述焉吾弗爲之矣君子

遵道而行半塗而廢吾弗

能已矣君子依乎中庸遯

世不見知而不悔唯聖者

能之君子之道費而隱夫

婦之愚可以與知焉及其

this I do not.

2.

The man of breed comes into harmony with the process and continues his
way. Go half way and then stop, I can't
let it go at that.

3.

The man of breed pivots himself on
the unchanging and has faith. To with-
draw from the world, unseen and unir-
ritated by being unseen, his knowledge
ignored: only the saint or the sage can
compass this.

PART TWO

TSZE SZE'S SECOND THESIS

XII

1.

The ethic of the man of breed im-
plies a great deal, but is not showy; it is
fecund, distributive, tranquil, secret and
minute.

2.

Quite humble or simple people can
participate in this ethic,

至也雖聖人亦有所不知
焉夫婦之不肖可以能行
焉及其至也雖聖人亦有
所不能焉天地之大也人
猶有所憾故君子語大天
下莫能載焉語小天下莫

but in its utmost not even the sage can know all of the process; the simple and sub-mediocre can follow some of the precepts, but in its utmost not even the sage can realize all of it. Great as are heaven and earth men find something to say against them in criticism; when the man of breed uses the word "great" he means something which nothing can contain; when he defines the minute he means something which nothing can split.

能破焉詩云鳶飛戾天魚

躍于淵言其上下察也君

子之道造端乎夫婦及其

至也察乎天地子曰道不

遠人人之爲道而遠人不

可以爲道詩云伐柯伐柯

3.

In the *Book of Poems* it is said:

The falcon comes out like a dog
From the high-arched gate of heaven;
The fish moves on wing-like foot
    in the limpid deep.

This is to evoke the thought of height and depth.

4.

The ethic of the man of high breed has its origin in ordinary men and women, but is, in its entirety, a rite addressed to heaven and earth.

This chapter refers to the phrase in the first chapter: "One does not depart from the process." There now follow eight chapters to back up this one.

XIII

1.

Kung said: The process is not far from man, it is not alien from him. Those who want to institute a process alien to mankind [at variance with human nature] cannot make it function as an ethical system.

2.

The *Book of Poems* says:

Cutting axe-handle
Cutting an axe-handle,
The model is not far off.

其則不遠執柯以伐柯睨
而視之猶以為遠故君子
以人治人改而止忠恕違
道不遠施諸己而不願亦
勿施於人君子之道四丘
未能一焉所求乎子以事

One seizes one axe-handle in cutting the other. One can, at a glance, note a divergence from the model. Thus the man of breed uses men in governing men. Having eliminated the defects, he stops.

3.

If a man have good will at his center [sympathy in his midheart] the process is not far from him: Do not to another what you would not like to have happen to you.

4.

The ethics of the man of true breed contain four things and I have not been able to perform one of them. I have not been able

父未能也所求乎臣以人事
君未能也所求乎弟以事
兄未能也所求乎朋友先
施之未能也庸德之行庸
言之謹有所不足不敢不
勉有餘不敢盡言顧行行

to serve my father as I would have a son serve me; nor my prince as I would have a minister serve me; nor to treat my elder brother as I would have a younger treat me; nor a friend as I would have a friend treat me. No. These things I have not attained to.

The honest man looks into himself and in his daily acts maintains constant respect to his given word that his deeds fall not below it. If he have failed in something, he dare not slacken in the attempt toward it; if he have erred, he dare not carry the error to the extreme; his words accord with his acts and his conduct

顧言君子胡不慥慥爾君
子素其位而行不願乎其
外素富貴行乎富貴素貧
賤行乎貧賤素夷狄行乎
夷狄素患難行乎患難君
子無入而不自得焉在上

with his words as of one who turns to compare them with scruple.

The essence of honesty is that it springs from the heart.

Tsze Sze's Second Thesis

XIV

1.

The man of breed looks at his own status, seeing it in clear light without trimmings; he acts, and lusts not after things extraneous to it.

2.

Finding himself rich and honored he behaves as befitting one who is rich and honored; finding himself of low estate he behaves as is fitting for a man of low estate; be he among barbarian tribes he acts as one should act where men and dogs sleep round the camp fire; in sadness and difficulty he acts as man should in sadness and straits. The man of breed can not be split in such a way as to be shut off and unable to rejoin himself.

3.

In high

位不陵下在下位不援上
正己而不求於人則無怨
上不怨天下不尤人故君
子居易以俟命小人行險
以徼幸子曰射有似乎君
子失諸正鵠反求諸其身

office he does not ill-treat his subordinates; in lower post he does not flatter his seniors. He corrects himself and seeks nothing from others, thus he is not disappointed; and has no resentments toward heaven above, nor rancors against other men here below.

4.

The man of probity is therefore calm and awaits his destiny. The small man takes risks, walking on the edge of the precipice, trying to fool his luck and outwit the hazard.

5.

Kung said: there is an analogy between the man of breed and the archer. The archer who misses the bulls-eye turns and seeks the cause of his failure in himself.

君子之道辟如行遠必自

邇辟如登高必自卑詩曰

妻子好合如鼓瑟琴兄弟

既翕和樂且耽宜爾室家

樂爾妻帑子曰父母其順

矣乎子曰鬼神之爲德其

XV

1.

In the honest man's ethic we find
analogy to the traveler to a far country:
he has first to cross the near; likewise to
the high climber who must first start at
the bottom.

2.

The *Book of Poems* says:
Union of affection with wife
                    and children
Is like the sound of drums and lutes,
The music of the sih *lute*
Measured by that of the ch'in *lute;*
The harmony between elder
                    and younger brother
Is like that at the holy altar
When the grain is offered up to the gods.
Bring your family thus into order
That you may have joy under your roof;
Therein is the treasure,
There are the silk and the gold.

　　　—*Shi King*, II, 1, 4, 7, 8.

The Ode beginning:
　　Glorious and abundant
　　The cherry trees are in flower
　　In all the world there is nothing
　　Finer than brotherhood.

3.

Kung said: The parents are in harmony, their wills harmonize, do they not?

*Translator's Note: I think he means that
the actual generative power is due precisely
to this harmony. Harmony of will and of
all else.*

129

盛矣乎視之而弗見聽之
而弗聞體物而不可遺使
天下之人齊明盛服以承
祭祀洋洋乎如在其上如
在其左右詩曰神之格思
不可度思矧可射思夫微

XVI

1.

Kung said: The spirits of the energies and of the rays have their operative *virtu*.

Tsze Sze's Second Thesis

The spirits of the energies and the rays are efficient in their *virtu*, expert, perfect as the grain of the sacrifice.

2.

We try to see them and do not see them; we listen and nothing comes in at the ear, but they are in the bones of all things and we can not expel them, they are inseparable, we can not die and leave them behind us.

3.

They impel the people of the whole empire to set in order and make bright the vessels for the sacred grain, to array themselves for the rites, to carry human affairs to the cognizance of the gods with their sacrifice, they seem to move above (the heads of the officiants) as water wool-white in a torrent, and to stand on their right hand and left hand.

4.

These verses are found in the *Odes:*

The thought of the multitude
Can not grasp the categories
Of the thoughts of the spirits
Circumvolving, but the tense mind
Can shoot arrows toward them.

—*Shi King*, III, 3, 2, 7.

之顯誠之不可揜如此夫
子曰舜其大孝也與德為
聖人尊為天子富有四海
之內宗廟饗之子孫保之
故大德必得其位必得其
祿必得其名必得其壽故

Intangible and abstruse
        the bright silk of the sunlight
Pours down in manifest splendor,
You can neither stroke
        the precise word with your hand
Nor shut it down under a box-lid.

XVII

1.

Kung said: Shun was a son in the great pattern, that is his glory; in knowing himself he was a sage and he acted on the clarity of his self-knowledge; for honors he had the Empire, possessing all inside the four seas; he offered the sacrifices in the ancestral temple and his descendents offered them there to him.

2.

One would say that having this capacity for seeing clearly into himself and thereby directing his acts, he perforce came to the throne, perforce had these high honors, perforce this enduring fame, and longevity.

天之生物必因其材而篤
焉故栽者培之傾者覆之
詩曰嘉樂君子憲憲令德
宜民宜人受祿于天保佑
命之自天申之故大德者
必受命子曰無憂者其唯

3.

From of old, Heaven, in creating things, of necessity concentrates their materials in them, with energy and in due proportions, and thence it comes that it nourishes the vigorous tree and fells that which is ready to fall.

4.

The *Book of Poems* says:
Our joy is the Honest Prince
Worthy of affection
Ornament of our culture
True hearted and a good magistrate.

His virtues have coordinated the people
And brought them into harmony
>   *with nature*
His happiness and prosperity
>   *are from heaven*
And he has nourished
>   *this heavenly fortune;*
He has augmented his destiny
And reinforced the beneficence
>   *of the elements.*
>   —*Shi King*, III, 2, 5, 1.
>   (Cf. Odyssey I, 34.)

5.

Who has this great power to see clearly into himself without tergivisation, and act thence, will come to his destiny (that is a high destiny).

XVIII

1.

Kung said: King Wen alone of men had no cause for regrets.

文王子以王季子為父以武
王為子父作之子述之武
王纘大王王季文王之緒
壹戎衣而有天下身不失
天下之顯名尊為天子富
有四海之內宗廟饗之子

His father was King Chi, his son Wu; the first laid the sound basis for the Empire and the second transmitted it with honor.

2.

King Wu completed the work of the Kings T'ai, Chi and Wen. He buckled on his armour but once, and with that once conquered the Empire, without losing his spotless reputation in the world. His title was "Son of Heaven," he had what lies within the four seas, he offered the sacrifices in the ancestral temple and his descendants maintained him with the same rites. So they nourished his spirit.

孫保之武王末受命周公
成文武之德追王大王王
季上祀先公以天子之禮
斯禮也達乎諸侯大夫及
士庶人父爲大夫子爲士
葬以大夫祭以士父爲士

3.

King Wu received the "Decree"
[was confirmed by heaven as Emperor]
in his old age; the Duke of Chou completed the just and splendid labors of the
Kings Wen and Wu, and established post-
humous titles for the Kings T'ai and Chi,
he honored the earlier Dukes with Imperial ceremonies, and extended the order
of ceremonies to the princes and great
officers, to the rest of the officers and
scholars and to the people. Thus if the
father was a grand officer and the son a
scholar, the funeral was of a grand officer
and the sacrifice that of a scholar; if the
father was a scholar

*Tsze Sze's
Second
Thesis*

子為大夫葬以士祭以大
夫期之喪達乎大夫三年
之喪達乎天子父母之喪
無貴賤一也子曰武王周
公其達孝矣乎夫孝者善
繼人之志善述人之事者

and the son a great officer the funeral was of a scholar and the sacrifice of a great officer.

Mourning for a great officer was for one year; for the Emperor three; in wearing mourning for one's father or mother there was no difference because of rank; in this noble and plebs were the same.

XIX

1.

Kung said: How high was the filial sense [sensibility] carried by King Wen and the Duke of Chou.

2.

Filial piety is shown in the rectitude and precision wherewith one executes the will and completes the work of one's forebears.

也春秋脩其祖廟陳其宗
器設其裳衣薦其時食宗
廟之禮所以序昭穆也序
爵所以辨貴賤也序事所
以辨賢也旅酬下為上所
以逮賤也燕毛所以序齒

3.

In the Spring and Autumn they set in order and adorned the sacred halls of their forebears. They set out the sacred vessels, donned the ceremonial robes and offered the sacred fruits of the season.

4.

With the rites in the ancestral temple they distinguished the degrees of the Imperial family, disposing the participants according to rank, they indicated also the worth of services rendered. The subalterns presented the cup in the general toast, and thus even the most humble had their part in the rites. In the banquets that followed the guests were arranged "according to hair" [as to color, i.e., according to age.]

也踐其位行其禮奏其樂

敬其所尊愛其所親事死

如事生事亡如事存孝之

至也郊社之禮所以事上

帝也宗廟之禮所以祀乎

其先也明乎郊社之禮禘

5.

They sat in the seats of their forebears, they followed their ceremonies,
they executed their classic music. They
honored those whom their forebears had
honored, showed love to those whom
their forebears had held in affection, and
greeted the dead as though they were
present in person.

Tsze Sze's
Second
Thesis

6.

With the rites to earth and heaven
they honored the God of Heaven; with
the ceremonies in the ancestral temples
they paid homage to their forebears.

嘗之義治國其如示諸掌
乎哀公問政子曰文武之
政布在方策其人存則其
政舉其人亡則其政息人
道敏政地道敏樹夫政也者
蒲盧也故爲政在人取人以

He who understands the meaning and the justice of the rites to Earth and Heaven will govern a kingdom as if he held it lit up in the palm of his hand.

DUKE NGAI'S QUESTION

XX

1.

The Duke Ngai asked about government.

2.

Kung replied: The government of Wen and Wu is clearly recorded on the square wooden tablets and on the strips of bamboo. Produce such men and a government will spring up in their style, forget such men and their form of government will shrivel.

3.

If men proceed in sane manner, government will spring up quickly, you will see how swift is the process of earth that causes straight plants to rise up; an eminent talent for government will cause government to rise as rushes along a stream.

> Pauthier notes that the bamboo is both hard and supple.

4.

Government is rooted in men, it is based on man. And one reaches men through oneself.

身脩身以道脩道以仁者
人也親親為大義者宜也尊
賢為大親親之殺尊賢之等
禮所生也在下位不獲乎上
民不可得而治矣故君子不
可以不脩身思脩身不可以

You discipline yourself with ethics, and ethics are very human; this *humanitas* is the full contents of man, it is the contents of the full man.

One orders a system of ethics with human qualities.

5.

This good will, *humanitas*, ethics, is man. The great thing is affection for relatives, the watching them with affection. Equity is something that springs up from the earth in harmony with earth and with heaven.

Translator's Note: The ideogram represents the sacrificial vase. Ethics are born from agriculture; the nomad gets no further than the concept of my sheep and thy sheep.

The great thing [in a system] is to render honor to the honest talent. The rites and forms of courtesy derive from the divers degrees of affection for our relatives and the proportionate honors due to the worthy.

6.

Legge rejects the next verse and Pauthier translates it: "If the subalterns have not the confidence of their superiors they cannot govern the people." Legge finds that this does not lead to verse 7.

The ideogram in dispute shows a hunting dog and a bird under the grass. The hunt-

149

不事親思事親不可以不知
人思知人不可以不知天天
下之達道五所以行之者三
曰君臣也父子也夫婦也
昆弟也朋友之交也五者
天下之達道也知仁勇三

*ing dog is a dog in whom one trusts, but he
is also a dog who trusts and has confidence
in the judgment of the hunter. As the
phrase recurs in verse* 17, *I translate it
tentatively in that place.*

7.

Thence the man of breed can not
dodge disciplining himself. Thinking of
this self-discipline he cannot fail in good
acts toward his relatives; thinking of
being good to his blood relatives he cannot skimp his understanding of nature
and of mankind; wanting to know mankind he must perforce observe the order
of nature and of the heavens.

8.

There are five activities of high im-
portance under heaven, and they are practiced with three virtues. I mean there are
the obligations between prince and minister; between father and son; between
husband and wife; between elder and
younger brothers; and between friends.
Those are the five obligations that have
great effects under heaven. The three efficient virtues are: knowledge, humanity
and energy;

者天下之達德也所以行
之者一也或生而知之或
學而知之或困而知之及
其知之一也或安而行之
或利而行之或勉強而行
之及其成功一也子曰好

and they are to be united in practice, do not attempt to split them apart one from the other.

9.

Some are born with instinctive knowledge, others learn by study, others are stupid and learn with great difficulty but the scope of knowing is one, it does not matter how one knows, the cult of knowledge is one.

Some proceed calmly setting themselves in harmony with the process [of nature, without doing violence to themselves] others behave well in the hope of profit, others forcing themselves against the grain, but the finished labor is one.

10.

Confucius said: Love

學近乎知力行近乎仁知
恥近乎勇知斯三者則知
所以脩身知所以脩身則
知所以治人知所以治人
則知所以治天下國家
矣凡為天下國家有九經曰

of study is near to knowledge; energy is near to benevolence; to feel shame is near to boldness.*

11.

He who knows these three (virtues) knows the means to self-discipline, he who can rule himself can govern others, he who can govern others can rule the kingdoms and families of the Empire.

12.

All who have families and kingdoms to govern have nine rules to follow, to wit:

---

* Intrepidity. Morrison says that the Chinese soldiers in the XIXth Century had this ideogram embroidered on the back and front of their jackets.

脩身也尊賢也親親也敬
大臣也體群臣也子庶民
也來百工也柔遠人也懷諸
侯也脩身則道立尊賢則
不惑親親則諸父昆弟不
怨敬大臣則不眩體群臣

to control themselves, to honor men of honest talent, to treat their relatives with affection, to respect the great ministers, to maintain the *esprit de corps* of the rest of the officers and officials, to treat the people as children, to attract the artisans of the hundred trades to the country, to show courtesy to those who come from afar, and to show tact in dealing with the princes and great feudal chiefs of the states.

13.

By self-discipline one establishes the model of conduct; by honoring and promoting honest men of talent one guards against being deceived [i.e. one sets up as a model men who do not try to show superlative cleverness in deceiving others]; kindness to relatives prevents rancor between the [imperial or royal] uncles and brothers; he who respects the great ministers will not be led astray by vain rumors [by false news]; maintaining the *esprit de corps*

則士之報禮重子庶已則
百姓勸來百工則財用足
柔遠人則四方歸之懷諸
侯則天下畏之齊明盛服
非禮不動所以脩身也去
讒遠色賤貨而貴德所以

among the officers civil and military will
conduce to their good conduct according
to custom; treating the mass of the people as children will mean that the "hundred families" [the whole people] will
stimulate each other [in good conduct]
from a simple tendency toward imitation;
attracting the artisans of the hundred
trades will mean that the empire's raw
materials will be utilized continually and
efficiently; courtesy to foreigners [mer-
chants, etc.] will bring them from the
four corners of the earth, and cordial
relations with the princes and feudatories
will have beneficent repercussions everywhere.

14.
    Discriminate; illuminate; use a-
bundantly all things available; do not
drive toward anything that is contrary
to the rites: these are the modes of self-
discipline, the instruments of self-discipline.

    Keep calumny afar off, get rid of
viscid show, hold material riches in low
esteem and in high esteem that conduct
which comes from the straight gaze into
the heart, from the inner clarity: that is
the way

勸賢也尊其位重其祿同

其好惡所以勸親親也官

盛任使所以勸大臣也忠

信重祿所以勸士也時使

薄斂所以勸百姓也日省

月試既廩稱事所以勸百

to stimulate worthy ministers; giving positions of honor and high salaries and sharing in their loves and hates is the way to lead the imperial relatives to treat you with parental affection; giving them plenty of subordinate officers properly and seriously to carry out confidential orders and missions of trust is the way to encourage the great ministers; cordial confidence and good pay are the means of keeping up the officers' *esprit de corps*; requiring service in due seasons only, and keeping the taxes light, is the way to encourage the people; daily supervision, monthly tests, food ration proportionate* to the work done, are the ways of encouraging

---

* The ideogram seems to indicate an order against the granary, a sort of mandate for grain, but may also contain the idea of giving the full pay as soon as the work is finished, not delaying the payment.

工也送往迎來嘉善而矜
不能所以柔遠人也繼絕
世舉廢國治亂持危朝聘
以時厚往而薄來所以懷
諸侯也凡為天下國家有
九經所以行之者一也凡事

the artisans; to go with the departing
a bit of their way, and to go out to meet
those who arrive, praise the capable,
have compassion on the incompetent, are
modes of establishing easy intercourse
with foreigners from afar; to continue
the line of succession in families where
the direct line fades out, to restore ruin'd
states, to bring order into confusions, to
give support to weak states in their times
of danger, taking hold of these perils well
beforehand, to receive personally their
ambassadors punctually at the appointed
hour, constitute the ways of maintaining
cordial relations with the great feudatories and chiefs.

15.
All those who have the government
of kingdoms and great families have these
nine rules to observe, not separately one
from another, but all together as a whole.

豫則立不豫則廢言前定
則不跲事前定則不困行
前定則不疚道前定則不
窮在下位不獲乎上民不
可得而治矣獲乎上有道
不信乎朋友不獲乎上矣

16.

In all affairs those which are calmly prepared make a solid base, those which are not prepared run to ruin before they are ripe; speeches calmly prepared are not empty, affairs thought out in tranquility are not sabotaged later, and you do not get tired in carrying them out; action well considered beforehand does not bring anguish and a well thought mode of action is not interrupted from internal causes, it goes on without blocking obstacles and constrictions.

17.

If there be not mutual trust between subalterns and their chief* you will not manage to govern the people. There is a way to obtain the confidence of one's superiors; if there be not fidelity to the given word between friends there will not be confidence between you and your chiefs;

---

* See note in place of verse 6, on the hunting dog.

信乎朋友有道不順乎親

不信乎朋友矣順乎親有

道反諸身不誠不順乎

矣誠身有道不明乎善不

道反諸身不誠不明乎

誠乎身矣誠者天之道也

誠之者人之道也誠者不

to attain confidence between friends there is a way or process to follow; if a man cannot get on with his relatives, his friends will not have confidence in him; there is a way to get on with your relatives; if, searching inside yourself, you cannot tell yourself the truth in plain words, you will not get on with your relatives; and for attaining this precision of speech with yourself there is a way; he who does not understand what the good is, will not attain a clear precision in defining himself to himself.

18.
   Sincerity, this precision of terms is heaven's process.
   What comes from the process in human ethics. The sincere man finds the axis without

勉而中不思而得從容中
道聖人也誠之者擇善而
固執之者也博學之審問
之慎思之明辨之篤行之
有弗學學之弗能弗措也
有弗問問之弗知弗措也

forcing himself to do so. He arrives at it without thinking and goes along naturally in the midst of the process [*Ts'ung yung chung tao*], he is a wise man. He who is sincere seizes goodness, gripping it firmly from all sides.

19.

He concentrates in a pervading study, searches benevolently as if he were watching over a rice field, he looks straight into his own thoughts, he clarifies the just distinctions [between one thing or category and another], and continues thus with vigor.

20.

If there is something he have not studied, or having studied be unable to do, he does not file it away in the archives; if there be a question he have not asked, or to which, after research, he have not found an answer, he does not consider the matter at an end;

有弗思思之弗得弗措也
有弗辨辨之弗明弗措也
有弗行行之弗篤弗措也
人一能之己百之人十能
之己千之果能此道矣雖
愚必明雖柔必強自誠明

if he have not thought of a problem, or, having thought, have not resolved it, he does not think the matter is settled; if he have tried to make a distinction but have not made it clear [as between things or categories] he does not sink into contentment; if there be a principle which he has been unable to put into practice, or if practicing, he have not managed to practice with energy or vigor, he does not let up on it. If another man gets there with one heave, he heaves ten times; if another succeed with a hundred efforts, he makes a thousand.

Duke Ngai's Question

21.

Proceeding in this manner even a fellow who is a bit stupid will find the light, even a weak man will find energy.

TSZE SZE'S THIRD THESIS

XXI

Intelligence that comes from sincerity

謂之性自明誠謂之教誠
則明矣明則誠矣唯天下
至誠為能盡其性能盡其
性則能盡人之性能盡人
之性則能盡物之性能盡
物之性則可以贊天地之

is called nature or inborn talent; sincerity produced by reason is called education, but sincerity [this activity which defines words with precision] will create intelligence as if carved with a knife-blade, and the light of reason will produce sincerity as if cut clean with a scalpel.

Tsze Sze takes up the theme of this 21st chapter and reaffirms it in the chapters that follow.

XXII

Only the most absolute sincerity under heaven can bring the inborn talent to the full and empty the chalice of the nature.

He who can totally sweep clean the chalice of himself can carry the inborn nature of others to its fulfillment; getting to the bottom of the natures of men, one can thence understand the nature of material things, and this understanding of the nature of things can aid

化育可以贊天地之化育

則可以與天地參矣其次致

曲曲能有誠誠則形形則

著著則明明則動動則變

變則化唯天下至誠爲能

化至誠之道可以前知國

the transforming and nutritive powers of earth and heaven [ameliorate the quality of the grain, for example] and raise man up to be a sort of third partner with heaven and earth.

XXIII

He who does not attain to this can at least cultivate the good shoots within him, and in cultivating them arrive at precision in his own terminology, that is, at sincerity, at clear definitions. The sincerity will begin to take form; being formed it will manifest; manifest, it will start to illuminate, illuminating to function, functioning to effect changes.

Only the most absolute sincerity under heaven can effect any change [in things, in conditions].

XXIV

In the process of this absolute sincerity one can arrive at a knowledge of what will occur. Kingdoms

家將興必有禎祥國家將
亡必有妖孽見乎蓍龜動
乎四體禍福將至善必先
知之不善必先知之故至
誠如神誠者自成也而道
自道也誠者物之終始不誠

and families that are about to rise will give, perforce, happy indications; kingdoms and families about to decay will give forth signs of ill augury. You look at the divining grass and at the turtle's shell; but look at the four limbs.

If ill fortune or good be on the way, one or the other, the good will be recognizable before hand, the ill will be evident before hand, and in this sense absolute sincerity has the power of a spiritual being, it is like a *numen*.

XXV

1.

He who defines his words with precision will perfect himself and the process of this perfecting is in the process [that is, in the process par excellence defined in the first chapter, the total process of nature].

2.

Sincerity is the goal of things and their origin, without this sincerity

無物是故君子誠之為貴

誠者非自成己而已也所

以成物也成己仁也成物

知也性之德也合外内之

道也故時措之宜也故至

誠無息不息則久久則徵

nothing is.

On this meridian the man of breed respects, desires sincerity, holds it in honor and defines his terminology.

3.

He who possesses this sincerity does not lull himself to somnolence perfecting himself with egocentric aim, but he has a further efficiency in perfecting something outside himself.

Fulfilling himself he attains full manhood, perfecting things outside himself he attains knowledge.

The inborn nature begets this activity naturally, this looking straight into oneself and thence acting. These two activities constitute the process which unites outer and inner, object and subject, and thence constitutes a harmony with the seasons of earth and heaven.

XXVI

1.

Hence the highest grade of this clarifying activity has no limit, it neither stops nor stays.

2.

Not coming to a stop, it endures; continuing durable, it arrives at the minima [the seeds whence movement springs].

徵則悠遠悠遠則博厚博

厚則高明博厚所以載物

也高明所以覆物也悠久

厚則高明所以覆物也悠

明配天悠久無疆如此者

所以成物也博厚配地高

不見而章不動而變無為

3.

From these hidden seeds it moves forth slowly but goes far and with slow but continuing motion it penetrates the solid, penetrating the solid it comes to shine forth on high.

4.

With this penetration of the solid it has effects upon things, with this shining from on high, that is with its clarity of comprehension, now here, now yonder, it stands in the emptiness above with the sun, seeing and judging, interminable in space and in time, searching, enduring, and therewith it perfects even external things.

5.

In penetrating the solid it is companion to the brotherly earth [offers the cup of mature wine to the earth] standing on high with the light of the intellect it is companion of heaven persisting in the vast, and in the vast of time, without limit set to it.

6.

Being thus in its nature; unseen it causes harmony; unmoving it transforms; unmoved

而成天地之道可壹言而
盡也其為物不貳則其生
物不測天地之道博也厚
也高也明也悠也久也今
夫天斯昭昭之多及其無
窮也日月星辰繫焉萬物

it perfects.

7.

The celestial and earthly process can
be defined in a single phrase; its actions
and its creations have no duality. [The
arrow has not two points].

There is no measuring its model for
the creation of things.

tse pu ts'e

8.

The celestial and earthly process per-
vades and is substantial; it is on high and
gives light, it comprehends the light and
is lucent, it extends without bound, and
endures.

9.

In the heavens present to us, there
shine separate sparks, many and many,
scintillant, but the beyond [what is beyond them] is not like a corpse in a shut
cavern.

Sun, moon and the stars, the sun's
children, the signs of the zodiac measuring the times, warners of transience, it
carries all these suspended, thousand on
thousand, looking down from above the
multitude of things created,

覆焉今夫地一撮土之多
及其廣厚載華嶽而不重
振河海而不洩萬物載焉
今夫山一卷石之多及其
廣大草木生之禽獸居之
寶藏興焉今夫水一勺之

it carries them, now here, now there, keeping watch over them, inciting them, it divides the times of their motions; they are bound together, and it determines their successions in a fixed order. The visible heaven is but one among many.

This earth that bears you up is a handful of sand, but in its weight and dusky large, it holds The Flower Mount and Dog Mountain without feeling the weight of them; Hoang Ho, the river, and the oceans surge and the earth loses not a drop of their waters, holding them in their beds, containing the multitude of their creatures.

Mount Upholder that you now look upon is but a fold of rock amid many, a pebble, and on its sides grow the grasses and trees, sheltering wild fowl and the partridge, the four-footed beasts and stags; gems are hidden within it abundantly that were for delight or for commerce.

This water is but a spoonful

多及其不測黿鼉鮫龍魚
鼈生焉貨財殖焉詩曰惟
天之命於穆不巳蓋曰天
之所以爲天也於乎不顯
文王之德之純蓋曰文王
之所以爲文也純亦不巳

mid many; it goes forth and in its deep
eddies that you can in no wise fathom
there be terrapin and great turtles, mon-
sters, crocodiles, dragons, fish and cru-
staceans to make rich whomso will seek
with a bold eye into their perils.

10.

The *Book of the Odes* says:

*The decree of heaven
          takes the bird in its net.
Fair as the grain white-bearded
There is no end to its beauty.*

The hidden meaning of these lines is:
thus heaven is heaven [or this is the
heavenly nature, co-involgent].

*As silky light, King Wen's virtue
Coming down with the sunlight,
                    what purity!
He looks in his heart
And does.*

—*Shi King*, IV, 1, 2, 1.

Here the sense is: In this way was Wen
perfect.

The *unmixed* functions [in time and
in space] without bourne.

This unmixed is the tensile light, the
          Immaculata. There is no end
                    to its action.

NOTE

Twenty-four centuries ago Tsze Sze needed to continue his comment with a profession of faith, stating what the Confucian idea *would* effect; looking back now over the millennial history of China there is need neither of adjectives nor of comment.

And for that reason I end my translation at this point, temporarily at least.

The dynasties Han, Tang, Sung, Ming rose on the Confucian idea; it is inscribed in the lives of the great emperors, Tai Tsong, Kao Tseu, Hong Vou, another Tai Tsong, and Kang Hi. When the idea was not held to, decadence supervened.

In the Occident Guicciardini wrote: "Nothing impossible to him who holds honor in sufficient esteem."

THE ANALECTS

PROCEDURE

The Root of Confucian teaching and its definition are given in The Adult Study (Confucius' summary and Tseng's comment) and the Pivot (Tsze Sze's three statements on Metaphysics, Politics and Ethics).

The Analects have no such coherence or orderly sequence; they are the oddments which Kung's circle found indispensable, and for 2,500 years the most intelligent men of China have tried to add to them or to subtract. After a milennium they found that Mencius' work could not be subtracted. And the study of the Confucian philosophy is of greater profit than that of the Greek because no time is wasted in idle discussion of errors. Aristotle gives, may we say, 90% of his time to errors, and the Occident, even before it went off for seven or more centuries into an otiose discussion of fads and haircuts (*vide* "The Venerable" Bede), had already started befuddling itself with the false dilemma: Aristotle OR Plato, as if there were no other roads to serenity.

Mencius never has to contradict Confucius; he carries the Confucian sanity down into particulars, never snared into rivalry by his flatterers.

Given the tradition that the Analects contain nothing superfluous, I was puzzled by the verses re length of the night-gown and the predilection for ginger. One must take them in the perspective of Voltaire's: "I admire Confucius. He was the first man who did *not* receive a divine inspiration." By which I mean that these trifling details were useful at a time, and in a world, that tended to myths and to the elevation of its teachers into divinities. Those passages of the Analects are, as I see it, there to insist that Confucius was a Chinaman, not born of a dragon, not in any way supernatural, but remarkably possessed of good sense.

He liked good music, he collected *The Odes* to keep his followers from abstract discussion. That is, *The Odes* give particular instances. They do not lead to exaggerations of dogma. Likewise he collected the *Historic Documents,* asserting, quite truly, that he had invented nothing. Without Kung no one would discover that his teaching, or at any rate the root and the seed, are there in the "History Classic."

The London *Times* has recently hit a new low in neglecting Kung's habit of summary. Anyone so unfortunate as to have the *Times'* critique of Kung's anthology thrust before them must, indeed, tingle with a slight warmth of irony. Kung said: "There are 300 Odes and their meaning can be gathered into one sentence: Have no twisty thoughts."

Some translators think of everything, positively of everything, save what the original author was driving at.

E. P.

Brief Concordance

Book   Chapter

Tactics I, 16.

No twisty thoughts: II, 2.

Government: II, 19; XII, 7; XII, 14; XIII, 1.

Veracity: II, 22; IX, 24.

Flattery: II, 24, I.

Arrangement of sequence of the ODES: IX, 14.

Men not horses: X, 12.

The Old Treasury: XI, 13.

VI, 11, cf/Agassiz.

The official: VI, 12.

man standing by his word

*respect for the kind of intelligence that enables grass
seed to grow grass; the cherry-stone to make cherries*

After Confucius' death, when there was talk of regrouping, Tsang declined, saying: "Washed in the Keang and Han, bleached in the autumn sun's-slope,* what whiteness can one add to that whiteness, what candour?" (Mencius III, 1; IV, 13.)

The friend who hoped to find beauty in this translation will not find the beauty of the Odes, nor the coherence of the Pivot. The Analects are neither a continuous narrative, nor a collection of fancy ideas. It is an error to seek aphorisms and bright saying in sentences that should be considered rather as definitions of words, and a number of them should be taken rather as lexicography, as examples of how Kung had used a given expression in defining a man or a condition.

Points define a periphery. What the reader can find here is a set of measures whereby, at the end of a day, to learn whether the day has been worth living. The translation succeeds in its moderate aim if it gives the flavour of laconism and the sense of the live man speaking.

After finishing it I turned back to Pauthier's French, and have included a number of his phrases as footnotes (marked P), sometimes as alternative interpretation, sometimes for their own sake even when I do not think he is nearer the original meaning.

The few dictionary references [M] *are to R. H. Mathews'* Chinese-English Dictionary *(Cambridge, Harvard University Press, 1947, 4th ed.), that being the one most easily obtainable at the moment.*

During the past half-century (since Legge's studies) a good deal of light has been shed on the subject by Fenollosa (Written Character as a Medium for Poetry), *Frobenius* (Erlebte Erdteile) *and Karlgren* (studies of sacrificial bone inscriptions).

E. P.

---

*yang[2]: bright, positive. Definite illustration of why one wants a bilingual edition. The usage of terms by any great stylist is, or should be, determined by the Four Books.

BOOK ONE
I

1. He said: Study with the seasons winging past, is not this pleasant?

2. To have friends coming in from far quarters, not a delight?

3. Unruffled by men's ignoring him, also indicative of high breed.

II

1. Few filial and brotherly men enjoy cheeking their superiors, no one averse from cheeking his superiors stirs up public disorder.

2. The real gentleman goes for the root, when the root is solid the (beneficent) process starts growing, filiality and brotherliness are the root of manhood, increasing with it.

III

1. He said: Elaborate phrasing about correct appearances seldom means manhood.

IV

1. Tseng-tse said: I keep an eye on myself, daily, for three matters: to get to the middle of mind when planning with men; to keep faith with my friends; lest I teach and not practice.

V

1. He said: To keep things going in a state of ten thousand cars: respect what you do and keep your word, keep accurate accounts and be friendly to others, employ the people in season. [*Probably meaning public works are not to interfere with agricultural production.*]

VI

1. He said: Young men should be filial in the home, and brotherly outside it; careful of what they say, but once said, stick to it; be agreeable to everyone, but develop friendship (further) with the real men; if they have any further energy left over, let them devote it to culture.

VII

1. Hsia-tze said: Gives weight to real worth and takes beauty lightly [or *"amid changing appearances"*], puts energy into being useful to his father and mother, and his whole personality into serving his prince; keeps his word with his friends; call him unaccomplished, I say that he is accomplished.

VIII

1. He said: A gentleman with no weight will not be revered, his style of study lacks vigour.

2. First: get to the middle of the mind; then stick to your word.

3. Friendship with equals.

4. Don't hesitate to correct errors.

IX

1. Tseng-tse said: Look clearly to the end, and follow it up a long way; the people acting on conscience will get back to the solid.

X

1. Tze-Chin asked Tze-Kung: When the big man gets to a country he has to hear about its government, does he ask for what's given him or is it just given?

2. Tze-Kung said: The big man is easy-going and kindly, respectful in manner, frugal, polite, that's how he gets it. His mode of going after it differs from other men's.

XI

1. He said: During a father's life time, do what he wants; after his death, do as he did. If a man can go along like his father for three years, he can be said to be carrying-on filially.

XII

1. Yu-tze said: Gentleness (easiness) is to be prized in ceremony, that was the antient kings' way, that was beautiful and the source of small actions and great.

2. But it won't always do. If one knows how to be easy and is, without following the details of ceremony, that won't do.

XIII

1. Yu-tze said: When keeping one's word comes near to justice one can keep it; when respect is almost a ceremony it will keep one far from shame and disgrace. Starting with not losing one's relatives, one can found a line with honour. [*This reading will be disputed and is perhaps too bold.*]

XIV

1. He said: A gentleman eats without trying to stuff himself, dwells without seeking (total) quietude, attends to business, associates with decent people so as to adjust his own decencies; he can be said to love study.

XV

1. Tze-King said: Poor and no flatterer, rich and not high-horsey, what about him?
He said: Not like a fellow who is poor and cheerful, or rich and in love with precise observance.
2. Tze-King said: It's in the Odes "as you cut and then file; carve and then polish." That's like what you mean?
3. Ts'ze here, one can begin to discuss the Odes with him; gave him the beginning and he knew what comes (after it).

XVI

1. He said: Not worried that men do not know me, but that I do not understand men.

BOOK TWO

I

1. Governing by the light of one's conscience is like the pole star which dwells in its place, and the other stars fulfill their functions respectfully.

II

1. He said: The anthology of 300 poems can be gathered into the one sentence: Have no twisty thoughts.

III

1. He said: If in governing you try to keep things leveled off in order by punishments, the people will, shamelessly, dodge.

2. Governing them by looking straight into one's heart and then acting on it (on conscience) and keeping order by the rites, their sense of shame will bring them not only to an external conformity but to an organic order.

IV

1. He said: At fifteen I wanted to learn.
2. At thirty I had a foundation.
3. At forty, a certitude.
4. At fifty, knew the orders of heaven.
5. At sixty was ready to listen to them.
6. At seventy could follow my own heart's desire without overstepping the t-square.

V

1. Mang-I-tze asked about filiality. He said: Don't disobey.*

2. Fan Ch'ih was driving him and he said: Mang-Sun asked me about filiality, I said: it consists in not disobeying (not opposing, not avoiding).

3. Fan Ch'ih said: How do you mean that? He said: While they are alive, be useful to them according to the proprieties, when dead, bury them according to the rites, make the offerings according to the rites.

VI

1. Mang Wu the elder asked about filiality. He said: A father or mother is only worried as to whether a child is sick.

VII

1. Tze-Yu asked about filiality. He said: Present day filial piety consists in feeding the parents, as one would a dog or a horse; unless there is reverence, what difference is there?

---

*P. expands the single word *wei* to mean: *s'opposer aux principes de la raison*, making the sentence equivalent to Gilson's statement of Erigena: Authority comes from right reason—anticipating the "rites" (light and dish of fecundity) a few lines further down.

VIII

1. Tze-Hsia asked about filiality. He said: The trouble is with the facial expression. Something to be done, the junior takes trouble, offers food first to his elders, is that all there is to filiality?

IX

1. He said: I have talked a whole day with Hui and he sits quiet as if he understood nothing, then I have watched what he does. Hui is by no means stupid.

X

1. He said: Watch a man's means, what and how.
2. See what starts him.
3. See what he is at ease in.
4. How can a man conceal his real bent?

XI

1. If a man keep alive what is old and recognize novelty, he can, eventually, teach.

XII

1. The proper man is not a dish.

XIII

1. Tze-Kung said: What is a proper man? He said: He acts first and then his talk fits what he has done.

XIV

1. He said: A proper man is inclusive, not sectary; the small man is sectarian and not inclusive.

XV

1. He said: Research without thought is a mere net and entanglement; thought without gathering data, a peril.

XVI

1. He said: Attacking false systems merely harms you.

XVII

1. He said: Yu, want a definition of knowledge? To know

is to act knowledge, and, when you do not know, not to try to appear as if you did, that's knowing.

XVIII

1. Tze-Chang was studying to get a paid job.

2. He said: Listen a lot and hide your suspicions; see that you really mean what you say about the rest, and you won't get into many scrapes. Look a lot, avoid the dangerous and be careful what you do with the rest, you will have few remorses. Salary is found in a middle space where there are few words blamed, and few acts that lead to remorse.

XIX

1. Duke Ai asked how to keep the people in order. He said: Promote the straight and throw out the twisty, and the people will keep order; promote the twisty and throw out the straight and they won't.

XX

1. Chi K'ang asked how to instill that sincere reverence which would make people work. He said: Approach them seriously [*verso il popolo*], respectful and deferent to everyone; promote the just and teach those who just cannot, and they will try.

XXI

1. Some one asked Confucius why he was not in the government.

2. He said: The Historic Documents say: filiality, simply filiality and the exchange between elder and younger brother, that spreads into government, why should one go into the government?

> [P. turns this admirably: Pourquoi considérer seulement ceux qui occupent des emplois publics, comme remplissant des fonctions publiques.]

XXII

1. He said: Men don't keep their word, I don't know what can be done for them: a great cart without a wagon-pole, a small cart and no place to hitch the traces.

1. Tze-Chang asked if there were any knowledge good for ten generations.

2. He said: Yin, because there was wisdom in the rites of Hsia, took over some and added, and one can know this; Chou because it was in the rites of Yin took some and added; and one can know what; someone will thread along after Chou, be it to an hundred generations one can know.

XXIV

1. He said: To sacrifice to a spirit not one's own is flattery.
2. To see justice and not act upon it is cowardice.

BOOK THREE

Pa Yih
The Eight Rows

I

1. Corps de ballet eight rows deep in Head of Chi's courtyard. Kung-tze said: If he can stand for that, what won't he stand for?

II

1. The Three Families used the Yung Ode while the sacrificial vessels were cleared away. He said: "The Princes are facing the Dukes, the Son of Heaven is like a field of grain in the sunlight," does this apply to their family halls?

III

1. A man without manhood, is this like a rite? Is there any music to a man without manhood?

IV

1. Lin Fang asked what was the root of the rites?
2. He said: That is no small question.
3. Better to be economical rather than extravagant in festivities and take funerals sorrowfully rather than lightly. [Poignancy rather than nuances (of ceremony).]

V

1.   He said eastern and northern tribes have princes not like this Hsia country has lost. [*Or:* which has lost them.]

VI

1.   The head of the Chi sacrificing to T'ai Shan (the Sacred East Mountain) Confucius said to Zan Yu: Can't you save him? The reply was: I cannot. Kung said: Too bad, that amounts to saying that T'ai Shan is below the level of Lin Fang. [*Vide supra,* IV, 1.]

VII

1.   He said: The proper man has no squabbles, if he contends it is in an archery contest, he bows politely and goes up the hall, he comes down and drinks (his forfeit if he loses) contending like a gentleman.

VIII

1.   Tze-Hsia asked the meaning of:
     "The dimpled smile, the eye's clear white and black,
       Clear ground whereon hues lie."
2.   He said: The broidery is done after the simple weaving.
3.   (Hsia) said: You mean the ceremonial follows . . .?
4.   He said: Shang's on, I can start discussing poetry with him.

IX

1.   He said: I can speak of the Hsia ceremonial but you can't prove it by Chi (data) ; I can speak of the Yin ceremonies but Sung (data) won't prove it. The inscribed offerings are insufficient to argue from, were they adequate they could bear me out. [*I should think this* hsien 4. M. 2699, *might refer to the inscribed sacrificial bones, which Karlgren has done so much work on.*]

X

1.   He said: When the Emperor has poured the libation in the Sacrifice to the Source of the dynasty, I have no wish to watch the rest of the service.

XI

1. Someone said: What does the sacrifice mean? He said: I do not know. If one knew enough to tell that, one could govern the empire as easily as seeing the palm of one's hand.

XII

1. He sacrificed as if he had taken root-hold in the earth, he sacrificed to the circumvolent spirits as if they took root.

2. He said: If I do not enter into this light, it is as if I did not sacrifice. [*Or*, if I do not give, *i.e.* myself, to it.]

XIII

1.   "stove versus altar"

Wang-sun Chia asked the meaning of: It is better to pay court to the hearth [*present lexicons*: stove] than to the mysterious (the household gods).

2. He said: It simply isn't. Who sins against heaven has nothing to pray to. [No means of getting light with the seasons.]

XIV

1. He said: Chou revised the two dynasties, how full and precise was its culture, I follow Chou.

XV

1. Entering the Great Temple he asked about every detail. Someone said: Who says the Man from Tsau knows the rites? He goes into the Great Temple and asks about everything. He said: That is the etiquette.

XVI

"bullseye better than shooting thru the target"

1. He said: In archery the going clean thru the leather is not the first requisite. Men aren't equally strong. That was the old way [? when they were expected to be all of them fit for it].

XVII

1. Tze-Kung wanted to eliminate the sheep from the sacrifice to the new moon.

2. He said: You, Ts'ze, love the sheep, I love the rite.

XVIII

1. He said: Some people consider it sycophancy to serve one's prince with all the details of the rites.

XIX

1. The Duke of Ting asked how a prince should employ his ministers, and how ministers should serve their prince. Kung-tze answered. The prince uses his ministers according to the prescribed ceremonial, ministers serve the prince by their sincerity. [The prince to judge the propriety, the ministers (middle-heart) not to fake in the execution.]

XX

1. He said: The fish-hawk song [*the first of the folk-songs in the anthology*] is pleasant without being licentious, its melancholy does no hurt (does not wound).

XXI

1. The Duke Ai asked Tsai Wo about the chthonian altars.* Tsai Wo replied: The Hsia dynasty's clans planted pines, the Yin cypress, and the men of Chou chestnut trees (*li*) in order to instill awe (*li*) in the populace.

2. Kung heard this and said: Perfect acts do not use words, prolonged customs are not sentenced, what formerly was is not to be blamed.

XXII

1. He said: Kwan Chung is a small dish, and how!
2. Someone said: Is Kwan Chung stingy?
3. He said: Kwan Chung had the Triple-Return (pagoda), court functionaries did not work overtime, how can he have been stingy?
4. "Did Kwan Chung, then, know the ceremonies?"
5. (He) said: Princes of States plant gate-screens; Kwan Chung also set up a gate-screen. When State-Princes meet they have a small table for inverted cups; Kwan also had a small table, if Kwan knew how to behave who doesn't?

---

*P. *autels ou tertres de terre*; rather than P's "*autour*", I should take "amid" pines, etc.

XXIII

1. Talking with the superintendent of music in Lu, he said:
One can understand this music; a rousing start in unison, then
the parts follow pure, clear one from another, (brilliant) explicit
to the conclusion.

XXIV

1. The Border Warden at I asked to see him, saying when
gentlemen come here I have always seen them. (Kung's) escort
introduced him. He came out saying: Small group of friends
[*lit*: you two three gentlemen] how can you regret his loss of office. The empire has long been in anarchy. Heaven will use the
big man as a watchman's rattle. [L. (*Legge*): bell with wooden
tongue. M.: with clapper.]

XXV

1. He said: The Shao (songs) are completely beautiful and
wholly good. The Wu are beautiful, completely, but not completely good (morally proportioned).

XXVI

1. He said: Dwelling on high without magnanimity, performing the rites without reverence, coming to funerals without
regrets; why should I bother about 'em?

BOOK FOUR

I

1. He said: A neighborhood's humanity is its beauty. If a
man doesn't settle among real people, how can he know.

II

1. He said: without manhood one cannot stand difficulties,
nor live for long amid pleasures. The real man is at rest in his
manhood, the wise man profits by it.

III

1. He said: only the complete man can love others, or hate
them.

IV

1. He said: if the will is set toward manhood, there is no criminality. [*The graph of* kou³ *suggests grass-root cf/mustard seed.*]

V

1. He said: Riches with honour are what men desire; if not obtained in the right way, they do not last. Poverty and penny-pinching are what men hate, but are only to be avoided in the right way.

2. If a gentleman give up manhood, what does his title really mean, what does the complete name gentle-man mean?

3. A proper man doesn't merely lay off his manhood after dinner. He must have it to make a sequence, he must have it in sudden disasters.

VI

1. He said: I have not seen anyone who loves whole-humanity and who hates un-whole manhood, if he love this whole-manhood (humanity) he cannot rise above it; if he hate the un-whole manhood, he would go to work on his own manhood, he would not try to get incomplete men to heighten his character for him.

2. If a man can direct his energy for one day toward manhood, eh? I have not seen anyone's energy insufficient.

3. A case may exist, but I have not seen it.

VII

1. He said: A man's errors, every one of em' belong to his environment (clique, party, gang he associates with), watch his faults and you can judge his humanity.

VIII

1. He said: hear of the process at sun-rise, you can die in the evening. [*Word order is:* morning hear process, evening die can? may, you may, it is possible that you may.]

IX

1. He said: A scholar with his will on learning the process,

206

who is ashamed of poor clothes, and fusses over bad food, is not worth talking to.

X

1. He said: a proper man is not absolutely bent on, or absolutely averse from anything in particular, he will be just.

XI

1. The proper man is concerned with examining his consciousness and acting on it, the small man is concerned about land; the superior man about legality, the small man about favours.

XII

1. He said: always on the make: many complaints.

XIII

1. He said: Can with ceremony and politeness manage a state, what difficulty will he have; unable to govern a state with ceremonies and courtesy; what ordered enlightenment has he?

XIV

1. He said: Not worried at being out of a job, but about being fit for one; not worried about being unknown but about doing something knowable.

XV

1. He said: Shan, my process is unified, penetrating, it holds things together and sprouts. Tsang said: Only?
2. (Kung)²-tze went out. A disciple asked: what does he mean? Tsang-tze said: the big man's way consists in sincerity and sympathy, and that's all.

XVI

1. He said: The proper man understands* equity, the small man, profits.

---

*yu: mouth answering in the affirmative, parable: responds to, all out for.

XVII

1. He said: See solid talent and think of measuring up to it; see the un-solid and examine your own insides.

XVIII

1. He said: In being useful to father and mother, one can almost reprove them; but if they won't do what one wants one must respect them and not oppose* them, work and not grumble.

XIX

1. He said: during their lifetime one must not go far abroad, or if one does, must leave an address.

XX

1. He said: To carry on in a father's way for three years, can be called continuing as a son.

XXI

1. He said: one must recognize the age of one's father and mother both as a measure of good, and of anxiety.

XXII

1. He said: The men of old held in their words for fear of not matching them in their character.

XXIII

1. Those who consume their own smoke seldom get lost. The concise seldom err.

XXIV

1. He said: the proper man wants to put a meaning into his words (or to be slow in speech), ready in action.

XXV

1. He said: candidness is not fatherless, it is bound to have neighbours.

XXVI

1. Tze-Yu said: Harping on things with a prince brings disgrace, and between friends estrangement.

---

*wei cf/II. v. 1.

BOOK FIVE

Kung-Ye Ch'ang

I

1. He described Kung-Ye Ch'ang as a suitable husband: although he was fettered with the black (criminal's) rope he was not guilty; completing the idea he gave him his daughter to wife.

2. Of Nan Yung he said: if the country were well governed he would not be out of office; if the country were in chaos he would escape punishment and disgrace; he gave him his elder brother's daughter to wife.

II

1. He said of Tze-Chien: a proper man, and how! If there weren't proper men in Lu, where did he get it from?

III

1. Tze-Kung said: What about me, Ts'ze? Confucius said: You're a dish. "What kind?" Confucius said: Oh, a jewelled one for the altar.

IV

1. Someone said: Yung is a full man but not eloquent. [Persuasive, *ideogram: man tranquillizing a woman.*]

2. He said: How would he use verbal cleverness? Resist men with glibness, it will get you constant detestations from them; how would he use clever talk?

V

On not wishing to be forced into insincerity

1. He was urging Ch'i-tiao to go into government employ, who answered: I couldn't keep my word (if I did). Confucius was pleased. [*Word order:* I this, or thus, is not can stand by my word.]

VI

1. He said: The process is not acted upon [*old style: "the way is not trodden"*]. I will get onto a raft and float at sea and . . .

eh . . . Yu will follow me. Tsze-lu (Yu) was pleased to hear this. Confucius said: Yu likes audacity more than I do, he wouldn't bother to get the logs (to make his raft).

VII

1. Mang Wu the elder asked if Tze-Lu was a whole man. Confucius said: I don't know.

2. He (Mang) asked again, and Confucius said: In a state of a thousand cars he could manage military enrollment, but I do not know if he is a total man.

3. "What about Ch'iu?" Confucius said: He could govern a city of a thousand families, or a clan mounting a hundred war cars, I do not know if he is all one can ask of a man.

4. "What about Ch'ih?" Confucius said: Ch'ih, in an immaculate sash, could be used to talk to visitors and court guests, I do not know if he is all one can ask of a man.

VIII

1. He asked Tze-Kung: who comprehends most, you or Hui?

2. The answer: No comparison, Hui hears one point and relates it to ten (understands its bearing on ten, I on one only); I hear one point and can only get to the next.

3. He said: Not the same, I agree you are not alike.

IX

1. Tsai Yu was sleeping in day-time. Confucius said: Rotten wood cannot be carved; a wall of dung won't hold plaster, what's the use of reproving him?

2. He said: When I started I used to hear words, and believe they would be acted on; now I listen to what men say and watch what they do. Yu has caused that adjustment.

X

1. He said: I do not see anyone constant. Someone answered: Shan Ch'ang. He said: Ch'ang is moved by his passions, how can he achieve constancy?

XI

1. Tze-Kung said: What I don't want done to me, I don't

want to do to anyone else. Confucius said: No, Ts'ze, you haven't got that far yet.

XII

1. Tze-Kung said: The big man's culture shows, one can manage to hear about that; the big man's words about the inborn-nature and the process of heaven, one cannot manage to hear. [They don't go in through the ear.]

XIII

1. When Tze-Lu had heard of anything he couldn't practice he was only worried about having heard it. [*Doubtful reading*].

XIV

1. Tze-Kung asked how Kung-Wan got to be called "Wan," the accomplished. Confucius said: He was active, loved study and was not ashamed to question his inferiors, therefore described as "the accomplished."

XV

1. He said to Tze-Ch'an: there are four components in a proper man's doing: He is reverent in his personal conduct, scrupulously honourable in serving his prince, considerate in provisioning the people, and just in employing them.

XVI

1. He said: Yen P'ing understood friendship, however long the intercourse his scruples remained as at first.

XVII

1. He said: Tsang Wan the elder kept a large tortoise; his capitals showed depicted mountains, and the little columns were adorned as if with duckweed; just what sort of knowledge had he? [*Legge's punctuation. Shift the comma and it cd/mean,* dwelt on Tsan (Tortoise) mountain.]

XVIII

1. Tze-Chang asked about Tsze-Wan made minister three times and his face showed no pleasure, retired three times and his face showed no displeasure, felt constrained to tell the new min-

ister about the old minister's (mode of) governing? Confucius said: a sincere man. (Chang) said: and as to his being the total man? Confucius said: I don't know how he can be called fully human.

2. Ch'ui-tze killed the Ch'i prince, Ch'an Wan had forty teams of horses, he abandoned them and went abroad, coming to another state he said: "They are like the great officer Ch'ui" and departed from that first state, to a second, and again saying: "They are like the great officer Ch'ui," he departed. What about him? Confucius said: pure. (Chang) said: total manhood? Confucius said: I do not know how this can amount to being total manhood.

XIX

1. Chi Wan thought three times before taking action. Confucius heard it and said: Twice might be enough.

XX

1. He said: Ning Wu when the country was well governed behaved as a savant; when the country was in chaos he acted as a simple rustic; one can attain this wisdom but not this simplicity.

XXI

1. When he was in Ch'an he said: Return, let me return. My associates are little children, uppish, shortcutters, versatile and accomplished up to the end of the chapter, but do not know how to moderate.

XXII

1. He said: Po-i and Shu-ch'i did not think about antient hates (birds hidden under the grass), you might say they moulted off their resentments.

XXIII

1. He said: Who calls Wei-shang Kao straight? Somebody begged a little vinegar, and he begged it from a neighbour and gave it him.

XXIV

1. He said: elaborate phrases and expression to fit [L. insin-

uating, pious appearance] self-satisfied deference; Tso Ch'iu-ming was ashamed of; I also am ashamed of 'em. To conceal resentment while shaking* hands in a friendly manner, Tso-Ch'iu-ming was ashamed to; I also am ashamed to.

XXV

1. Yen Yuan and Tze Lu were with him, he said: Let each of you say what he would like.

2. Tze-Lu said: I would like a car and horses, and light fur clothes that I could share with my friends. They could spoil 'em without offense.

3. Yen Yuan said: I should like goodness without aggressiveness and to put energy into doing a good job without making a show of it.

4. Tze-Lu said: Now, boss, I should like to hear your bent. Confucius said: that the aged have quiet, and friends rely on our words, and that the young be cherished.

XXVI

1. He said: is this the end of it? I have seen no one who can see his errors and then go into his own mind and demand justice on them in precise, just, discriminating words.

XXVII

1. He said: a village with ten homes will contain sincere men who stand by their word quite as well as I do, but no one so in love with study.

BOOK SIX

I

1. He said: Yung could be appointed to a throne [*idiom: south face*].

2. Ching-kung asked about Tze-sang Po-tze. Confucius said: Can do. [Able, handy.]

3. Chang-kung said: if a man's home address is reverence

---

*This is the picture, L. and P. stick to the dictionary simply, *appearing friendly.*

he can be easy going, and thereby come near the people, that's permissible? But if his basic address is: take it easy and he carries that into action, it will be too much of a take-it-easy.

4. Confucius said: Yung has the word for it.

> [*Note: the terminology in some of these very short verses must be discussed between students, no one version can be just swallowed.*]

II

1. The Duke Ai asked which of the young fellows loved study.

2. Confucius replied: There was Yen Hui who loved to study, he didn't shift a grudge or double an error [L. repeat a fault]. Not lucky, short life, died and the pattern is lost, I don't hear of anyone who likes study.

III

1. Tze Hwa was commissioned to Ch'i, Mr. Zan asked grain for his mother. He said: give a fu. He asked for more. He said give a bushel. Zan gave five ping. [*L. note figures it may have been the whole of his own grain allowance.*]

2. Ch'ih was going to Ch'i, with a team of fat horses, and wearing light fox fur, I have heard that gentlemen aid the distressed, not that they tie up with riches. [L.M.: add to wealth of rich.]

3. Yuan Sze being made governor, declined 900 measures of grain given him.

4. Confucius said: Don't, they could be given to your big and little hamlets, villages, towns.

IV

1. He said in reference to Ching-kung: if the spotted cow's calf be red with the right sort of horn, though men won't want to use it, will the mountains and rivers reject it?

V

1. He said: Hui, now, a mind that for three months wouldn't

214

transgress humanity; the rest of 'em, can reach this pattern for a day or a month, and that's all. [*L. probably better*: get to it in a day or a moon, and that's all, *i.e.*, get there but not stick.]

VI

1. Chi K'ang asked if Chung-yu could be appointed as colleague in government. Confucius said: Yu's a determined fellow, what would be the trouble about his carrying on the government work? (K'ang) asked if Ts'ze could be given a government appointment. Said: Ts'ze's intelligent (penetrating) why not? (K'ang) said: and Ch'iu? Said: Ch'iu's versatile, what's against his doing government work?

VII

(On declining to serve an evil overlord.)

1. The Head of Chi appointed Min Tze-chien governor of Pi. Min Tze-chien said: Kindly decline for me, and if they come, back for me I shall have to (go) live up over the Wan.

VIII

1. Po-niu was ill. Confucius went to ask after him and took hold of his hand through the window. Said: he's lost, it is destiny, such a man, and to have such a disease. Such a man, such a disease.

IX

1. He said: Hui had solid talent (merit). One bamboo dish of rice, one ladle full of drink, living in a wretched lane, others couldn't have stood it. Hui continued to enjoy (life) unaltered, that's how solid his talent was.

X

1. Yen Ch'iu said: It's not that I don't like your system, I haven't the strength for it. He said: If a man isn't strong enough he stops half way, you shut yourself in (draw your own limit. M. 2222).

XI

1. He said to Tze-Hsia: Observe the phenomena of nature

as one in whom the ancestral voices speak, don't just watch in a mean way.

XII

1.   When Tze-Yu was governor of Wu-ch'ang, he said to him: Got any men there, what about 'em? Answered: Got Tan-t'ai Mieh-ming who never takes a short cut and never comes to my office except when he has government business.

XIII

1.   He said: Mang Chih-fan doesn't brag. He was in the rear of a retreat, but when nearing the (city) gate, whipped up his horse and said: not courage keeping me back, horse wouldn't go.

XIV

1.   He said: if you haven't the smooth tongue of T'o the prayer-master, or Sung Chao's beauty, it's hard to get away with it in this generation.

XV

1.   He said: The way out is via the door, how is it that no one will use this method.

XVI

1.   He said: More solidity than finish, you have the rustic; more finish than solid worth, the clerk; accomplishment and solidity as two trees growing side by side and together with leafage and the consequence is the proper man.

XVII

1.   He said: men are born upright, if they tangle this inborn nature, they are lucky to escape.

XVIII

1.   He said: Those who know aren't up to those who love; nor those who love, to those who delight in.

XIX

1.   He said: One can talk of high things (or, of the better

things) with those who are above mediocrity, with those below mediocrity one cannot.

XX

1. Fan Ch'ih asked about knowing. He said: put your energy into human equities, respect the spirits and powers of the air and keep your distance, that can be called knowing. He asked about humanitas. (Confucius) said: the real man goes first for the difficulty, success being secondary. That you can call manhood.

XXI

1. He said: the wise delight in water, the humane delight in the hills. The knowing are active; the humane, tranquil; the knowing get the pleasure, and the humane get long life.

XXII

1. He said: If Ch'i could make one change it would come up to Lu; if Lu could achieve one change it would arrive at the right way to do things.

XXIII

1. He said: a cornered dish without corners; what sort of a cornered dish is that?

XXIV

1. Tsai Wo said: If you yell: "well-hole" [*Both L. and M. say: meaning, "a man down it"*], will the proper man go down after him? He said: why? a proper man would come to the edge, he can't (be expected to) sink; he can be cheated, but not entrapped.

> [It is not up to him to go down it. *Why not the literal:* If they tell him manhood is at the bottom of the well, will he go down after it? *a simple pun on the spoken word* jen² *without the graph.*]

XXV

1. He said: A proper man extends his study of accomplishment, he brings it into close definition for the rites, and that may

enable him to keep from divagations (from overstepping the edge of the field).

XXVI

1. He went to see (the duchess) Nan-tze. Tse-Lu was displeased. The big man said: Well I'll be damned, if there's anything wrong about this, heaven chuck me.

XXVII

1. He said: the pivot that does not wobble (what it's all about, always); looking into the mind and then doing; attain this? Few men have for long.

XXVIII

1. Tze-Kung said: if a man extend wide benefits to the people and aid them all [*pictorially:* sees that they all get an even or constant water supply] would you call that manhood? He said: why attribute that to manhood, he would have to be a sage, Yao and Shun were still worried about such things. [*Or:* at fault, unable to accomplish all that.]

2. The complete man wants to build up himself in order to build up others; to be intelligent (see through things) in order to make others intelligent.

3. To be able to take the near for analogy, that may be called the square of humanitas, and that's that.

BOOK SEVEN

Shu Erh

I

1. He said: Transmitting not composing, standing by the word and loving the antient [L. antients]. I might get by in old P'ang's class.

II

1. He said: like a dog by a spent camp-fire (i.e., silent or dark) remembering, studying and not satiate [*pictogrammically same dog under shelter. The "remembering" is specifically keep-*

ing the right tone of the word. Various signs containing dog cover the various emotions of dog in given conditions, and are oriented by context], teaching others without being weary, how can these things apply to me?

III

1. He said: To see into one's mind and not measure acts to it; to study and not analyse [*rt/hand component also in verb "to plough"*], to hear equity and not have the gumption to adjust (oneself to it), to be wrong and unable to change, that's what worries me.

IV

1. When dining at home, he was unbent, easy-like, with a smile-smile. [*P. charmingly; ses manières étaient douces et persuasives! que son air etait affable et prévenant!*]

V

1. He said: deep my decadence, I haven't for a long time got back to seeing the Duke of Chou in my dreams.

VI

1. He said: keep your mind (will, directio voluntatis) on the process (the way things function).
2. Grab at clarity in acting on inwit as a tiger lays hold of a pig.
3. That outward acts comply with manhood.
4. Relax in the cultural arts.

VII

1. He said: from the fellow bringing his flitch of dried meat upward, I have never refused to teach (anyone).

VIII

1. He said: not zeal not explain [*slightly more inclusive than L.'s I do not explain to anyone who is not eager*], not wishing to speak, not manifesting. [*L. M. slant it to equivalents of: I don't show it to anyone who won't put his own cards on the table.*] I hold up one corner (of a subject) if he cannot turn the other three, I do not repeat (come back to the matter).

IX

1. When eating beside someone in mourning he did not stuff himself.

2. He did not sing on the same day he had mourned.

X

1. He said to Yen Yuan: When in office keep to the edge of its duties; when out, don't meddle (keep under the grass), only I and you have this sense.

2. Tze-Lu said: if you were in charge of the three army corps whom would you take for associate?

3. He said: Not someone who would tackle a tiger bare-handed or cross a stream without boats and die without regret. Not on the staff; but a man who keeps both eyes open when approaching an action, who likes to plan and bring to precision.

XI

1. He said: If I could get rich by being a postillion I'd do it; as one cannot, I do what I like.

XII

1. The things he looked very straight at, were the arrangement of altar dishes, war and disease.

XIII

1. In Ch'i he heard the "Shao" sung, and for three months did not know the taste of his meat; said: didn't figure the performance of music had attained to that summit.

XIV

1. Yen Yu said: is the big man for the Lord of Wei? Tze-Kung said: I'll ask him.

2. Went in and said: What sort of chaps were Po-i and Chu-Ch'i? Confucius said: Antients of solid merit.

"(Did they) regret it?"

(Confucius) said: they sought manhood, and reached manhood, how could they regret after that?

(Tze-Kung) came out and said: He's not for him. (No go. Not business, won't work.)

XV

1. He said: a meal of rough rice to eat, water, to drink, bent arm for a pillow, I can be happy in such condition, riches and honours got by injustice seem to me drifting clouds.

XVI

1. He said: If many years were added to me, I would give fifty to the study of The Book of the Changes, and might thereby manage to avoid great mistakes.

XVII

1. [L.: What he constantly talked of, *but ya³ means also* elegant.] He frequently spoke of (and kept refining his expression about) the Odes, the Historic Documents, the observance of rites (ceremonial, correct procedure) all frequently (or polished) in his talk.

XVIII

1. The Duke of Sheh asked Tze-Lu about Confucius; Tze-Lu did not answer.

2. He said: Couldn't you have said: He's so keen and eager he forgets to eat, so happy he forgets his troubles and doesn't know age is coming upon him?

XIX

1. He said: I wasn't born knowing; love antiquity (the antients), actively investigating.

XX

1. He did not expatiate on marvels, feats of strength, disorder or the spirits of the air.

XXI

1. He said: three of us walking along, perforce one to teach me, if he gets it right, I follow, if he errs, I do different.

XXII

1. He said: Heaven gave me my conscience, what can Hwan T'ui do to me.

XXIII

1. He said: You two or three, do I hide anything from you? I do not hide anything from you, I don't go along and not give it you, that's me. (You are getting the real Ch'iu, Confucius-Hillock.)

XXIV

1. He taught by four things: literature, procedure, sincerity (middle-heart) and standing by his word. [P. *rather better*: employait quatre sortes d'enseignements. Taught by means of four things.]

XXV

1. He said: I have not managed to see a sage man. If I could manage to see a proper man (one in whom the ancestral voices function) that would do.

2. He said: A totally good man, I have not managed to see. If I could see a constant man (consistent, a "regular fellow") that would do.

3. To lack and pretend to have, to be empty and pretend to be full, to be tight and pretend to be liberal: hard to attain consistency (in that case).

XXVI

1. He fished but not with a net; shot but not at sitting birds.

XXVII

1. If there are men who start off without knowledge, I don't. I listen a lot and pick out what is balanced, see a lot and keep the tone of the word, and so manage to know.

XXVIII

1. It was bothersome to talk with Hu-hsiang folk, the disciples were worried when Kung received a boy.

2. He said: I give to those who approach, not to those who go away; who is so deep; if a man wash and approach, I give to the clean (or, to his cleanliness) I don't uphold his past (or his future).

XXIX

1. He said: Manhood, how is it something afar off; I want to be human, and that humanity I get to.

XXX

1. The Minister of Crimes in Ch'an asked Confucius if the Duke Chao knew the correct procedure. Confucius said: he knew the procedure.

2. Confucius went out, and (the Minister) beckoned to Wu-ma Ch'i saying: I hear the gentleman is not prejudiced (partisan) yet he is partisan. The prince married a Wu, of the same surname as (himself) and called her Wu-elder. If that's knowing proper procedure, who don't know procedure?

3. Wu-ma Ch'i reported this. Confucius said: Ch'iu's lucky (i.e., I am lucky). If I make a mistake it's bound to be known.

XXXI

1. If he was with a man who sang true, he would make him repeat and sing in harmony with him.

XXXII

1. He said: I am about up to anyone else in education, it's the personal conduct of a proper man, that's what I don't come up to.

XXXIII

1. He said: As sage, as full man, can I set myself up as a model? I try and don't slack when tired, I teach men without weariness, that's the limit of what you can say of me. Kung-hsi Hwa said: Exactly what we younger chaps can't get by study.

XXIV

1. He was very ill. Tze-Lu asked to pray. He said: Does one? Tze-Lu answered: one does. The Eulogies say: We have prayed for you to the upper and lower spirits venerable. He said: I, Ch'iu, have been praying for a long time.

XXXV

1. He said: extravagance is not a pattern for grandsons;

parsimony is pattern of obstinacy; better be obstinate than break the line to posterity.

XXXVI

1. He said: the proper man: sun-rise over the land, level, grass, sun, shade, flowing out; the mean man adds distress to distress.

XXXVII

1. He was both mild and precise; grave and not aggressive, reverent and tranquil.

BOOK EIGHT

T'ai Po

I

1. He said of T'ai Po: It can be said that he completely brought his acts up to the level of his inwit; three times refusing the empire, the people could not arrive at weighing the act.

> *Note: T'ai Po abdicated in favour of his younger brother, Wan's father, in order that Wan might inherit. This because he considered Wan the member of the family capable of delivering the state from the Yin dynasty.*

[*Syntactical trouble re/*"*three times.*" *Wan's father was the third son. The three might mean "in three ways"; for himself, his second brother, and their heirs?*]

II

1. He said: respect without rules of procedure becomes laborious fuss; scrupulosity without rules of procedure, timidity (fear to show the thought); boldness without such rules breeds confusion; directness without rules of procedure becomes rude.

2. Gentlemen "bamboo-horse" to their relatives [*The bamboo is both hard on the surface and pliant*] and the people will rise to manhood; likewise be auld (acquaintance) not neglected, the people will not turn mean (pilfer).

III

1.   Tsang-tze was ill; called his disciples saying: uncover my feet, my hands, the Odes say: cautious, tread light as on the edge of a deep gulph, or on thin ice.   And now and for the future I know what I am escaping, my children.

IV

1.   Tsang-tze was ill, Mang Chang-tze went to enquire.

2.   Tsang said: When a bird is about to die, its note is mournful, when a man is about to die, his words are balanced.

3.   There are three things a gentleman honours in his way of life: that in taking energetic action he maintain a calm exterior at far remove from over-bearing and sloth, that his facial expression come near to corresponding with what he says, that the spirit of his talk be not mean nor of double-talk.   The sacrificial covered splint fruit baskets and altar platters have assistants to look after them.

V

1.   Tsang-tze said: Able yet willing to ask those who were not talented, possessed of many things, but enquiring of those who had few, having as though he had not, full and acting as if empty, not squabbling when offended, I once had a friend who followed that service.

VI

1.   Tsang-tze said: Fit to be guardian of a six cubits orphan (a prince under 15) in governing a state of an hundred *li* who cannot be grabbed by the approach of great-tallies [ta chieh 795 (e) 6433.30 *must mean something more than L's "any emergency," i.e., must indicate not getting rattled either at nearing the annual report to the overlord, or by the coming near it, i.e., to the chance of appropriating to himself the symbol of power*] a proper man? aye, a man of right breed.

VII

1.   Tsang-tze: An officer cannot lack magnanimous courage (boldness of bow-arm) he carries weight on a long journey.

2. Full manhood in fulfilling his personal duties, is that not weighty, death and then it ends, is not that long?

VIII

1. He said: Aroused by the Odes.
2. Stablished by the rites.
3. Brought into perfect focus by music.

IX

1. He said: People can be made to sprout (produce, act, follow) they cannot be commissioned to know.

X

1. He said: In love with audacity and loathing (sickened at) poverty: (leads to) confusion; when a man's lack of manly qualities is excessively deep that also means disorder.

XI

1. He said: Though a man have the Duke of Chou's brilliant ability, if he be high-horsey and stingy, the rest is not worth looking at.

XII

1. He said: It is not easy to study for three years without some good grain from it.

> [*Ideogram* ku; *interesting as meaning both corn and good, or good luck.*]

XIII

1. He said: strong and faithfully loving study [strong, *again the "bamboo-horse"*: hard and supple] maintaining till death the balanced, radiant process.
2. As for looking for troubled waters to fish in. Not enter a province on the brink, nor live in a disorganized province; when the empire has the process (is functioning) will be looked at; when it is without organization, will be out of sight.
3. When a state is functioning, poverty and meanness are shameful; when a state is in chaos (ill governed) riches and honours are shameful. [*Let us say:* under a corrupt government.]

XIV

1. He said: not being in (an) office; not plan its functioning.

XV

1. He said: when Music Master Chih began [L. entered office] the ensemble finale of the fish-hawk song, came wave over wave an ear-full and how!

XVI

1. He said: Uppish and not straight, ignorant and dishonest, [*let us say*: not spontaneous], quite simple and still not keeping their word; I don't make 'em out. [Empty-headed, and not keeping their word.]

XVII

1. He said: study as if unattainable, as if fearing to lose (grip on it).

XVIII

1. He said: lofty as the spirits of the hills and the grain mother, Shun and Yu held the empire, as if not in a mortar with it. [M. 7615, e: as if unconcerned.]

XIX

1. He said: How great was Yao's activity as ruler lofty as the spirits of the hills; only the heavens' working is great, and Yao alone on that pattern, spreading as grass, sunlight and shadow, the people could not find it a name.

2. How marvellous the way he brought his energies to a focus. Brilliant-gleaming? the perfect expression of his statutes.

XX

1. Shun had five men [*emphasis on "men", I think*] for ministers and the empire was governed.

2. King Wu said: I have ten able ministers [*vide* L. *and* M. 4220. a 3.]. [*Unorthodox reading*: King Wu said: I have ten men to serve me in this chaos. M. 4220. 27. I have ten obstreperous, wrong-headed ministers.]

3. Kung-tze said: Talents are really hard to find. The houses of T'ang (Yao) and Yu (in the person of Shun). At the

time of (Yao of the house of) T'ang and (Shun of) Yu in their
plenitude, there was a woman and nine men only.

4. Having two thirds of the empire, by keeping them in service (in the uniform) of Yin, the conscientiousness of Chou can
be said to have attained its maximum in action.

XXI

1. He said: I find Yu without flaw, frugal in drinking and
eating, showing the utmost filial continuity with the spirits and
powers of air, badly dressed ordinarily, but absolutely elegant in
sacrificial black and blue robes and sovran-cap (mortar board),
an inferior palace for a house, he put all his energy into the irrigation and drainage (aqueducts and ditches), I find him utterly
flawless.

BOOK NINE

Tze Han

I

1. He seldom spoke of profits, destiny, and total manhood.

II

1. A villager from Ta-Hsiang said: Great man, Kung-tze
extends his studies but does nothing to bring his reputation to a
point.

2. Confucius heard this and asked his young students: what
should I do, take up charioteering or take up archery? I'll take
up charioteering.

III

1. He said: The ceremonial hemp cap is now silk; that's an
economy, I conform.

2. Bowing as you enter the hall is according to the rites, they
now bow when they have come up the hall, cheeky; although
against the common usage, I conform [or continue (to bow)] at
the lower end of the hall.

IV

1.   He was cut off from four things; he had no prejudices, no categoric imperatives, no obstinacy or no obstinate residues, no time-lags, no egotism.

V

1.   He was alarmed in Kwang.

2.   Said: King Wan has passed on, the wan (the precise knowledge) is rooted here?

3.   If heaven were about to destroy that spirit of precision, after Wan's death, it would not have lasted on and been given to me.   If heaven is not about to destroy that spirit, what are the people of Kwang to me?   [L.: what can they do to me?]

VI

1.   A great minister said to Tze-kung: your big man is a sage, how versatile he is.

2.   Tze-kung said: Aye, by heaven's indulgence is almost a sage, and also very versatile.

3.   Confucius heard, and said: does the great minister know me?   I was poor when young and therefore can do many things, humble jobs.   Need a proper man, a gentleman, be versatile?   He need not.

4.   Lao says He said: I was not trained (educated to the examinations) * and therefore learned the various arts.

VII

1.   He said: How do I grasp knowledge?   I am not wise, but if a plain man ask me, empty as empty [like? work in a cave?], [L:] I set it forth from one end to the other and exhaust it.

[*"Knock at double,"* or at both starts or principles, suggests the *meaning:* investigate the paradox, or the two principles, the conjunction, apparent contradiction, and then exhaust the question.]

VIII

1.   He said: the miracle bird has not arrived, the river gives forth no map (of turtle-shell), I've only myself to rely on.

---

*L.: having no official job.

IX

1. Seeing anyone in mourning or in full ceremonial dress and cap, or a blind man (one of the blind musicians) even though they were young he would rise, or, passing, pass quickly.

X

1. Yen Yuan sighed heavily and said: I looked up, they filled the aloft; I bored in to them and they were totally solid; respectfully standing before them, they suddenly took root-hold in consequence.

2. The big man, orderly, one point tied to another, with perfect balance induces men (words that grow as easily as weed, but are good, grain-words), he enlarges us with literature, and keeps us in bound by the rites.

> *"Rites"*: *This word* li³ *contains something of the idea in the french* "il sait vivre," *though it would be an exaggeration to say that one can always render it by that phrase.*

3. Wishing to finish, I cannot; having exhausted my talent, it is as if something was built up lofty; although I wish to comply with it, there is no way (to do so completely) (branch causes stop).

XI

1. He was very ill, Tze-Lu wanted the students to act as ministers.

2. In an interval of the fever He said: Yu (Tze-lu) has been being too-clever for a long time, whom would I fool by pretending to have ministers when I haven't: fool heaven?

3. Wouldn't it be better to die among two or three intimates than in ministers' hands? Might not have a big funeral, but I wouldn't just die in a ditch [*lit:* going along a road].

XII

1. Tze-kung said: I have a beautiful gem here; put it in a case and hoard it, or try to get a good price and sell it? He said: sell it, sell it, I wait for its price.

XIII

1. He was wanting to live among the wild tribes.

2. Someone said: Rough, vulgar, how do you mean? He said: if the right kind of man lived there, how would they stay so?

XIV
(Arrangement of the Song book)

1. He said: From Wei I came back to Lu and the music was put in order, the Elegantiae and the Lauds were each put in its proper place.

XV

1. He said: In public to be useful to the Dukes and Ministers, in private to be useful to one's father and elder brothers, not daring to neglect the service of dead; not to be obstinate with drink; how does this apply to me?

XVI

1. Standing on a river-bank he said: it is what passes like that, indeed, not stopping day, night.

XVII

1. I do not see love of looking into the mind and acting on what one sees there to match love of someone having beauty.

XVIII

I do not in the least understand the text of this chapter. Only guess at it I can make is:

1. He said: As a mountain (grave-mound) is not made perfect by one basket of earth; yet has position, I take position. If you dump one basket of earth on a level plain it is a start (toward the heap?), I make that start.

> *The chapter might conceivably refer to determining the proper site for a tumulus even if one could not complete it. L. unsatisfied as to meaning, and P. unsatisfactory.*

XIX

1. He said: Never inert in conversation, that was Hui.

XX

1. He described Yen Yuan: Alas, I see him advance, I never see him stop (take a position).

> *Putting the accent on the* hsi (2-5), *"a pity?" as Legge does not.*
>
> *There is no more important technical term in the Confucian philosophy than this* chih (3) *the hitching post, position, place one is in, and works from. Turn back also to the difficult chap. xviii. above.*

XXI

1. He said: There are sprouts that do not flower; flowers that come not to fruit, oh yes.

XXII

1. He said: You can respect 'em soon after birth, how can one know what will come up to present record; at forty or fifty and not heard (or if they don't hear sense) that (maturity) just isn't enough to respect.

XXIII

1. He said: can one help agreeing with talk of sound doctrine? It's the altering to enact that matters; can one fail to be pleased with south-east gentleness of discourse, it's the elucidation that matters. To be pleased and not elucidate (not understand), to assent but not act on. I just don't know how to take (that sort).

XXIV

1. He said: put first getting to the centre of the mind, and keeping one's word; no friends not like one; when a mistake is made, not fearing to change.

XXV

1. He said: the commander of three army corps can be kidnapped, you cannot kidnap a plain man's will.

XXVI

1. Standing by a man dressed in furs, unembarrassed, Yu could do that?

232

2. No hates, no greeds, how can he use evil means?

3. Tze-lu kept repeating this to himself. Confucius said: How can that be enough for complete goodness?

XXVII

1. He said: when the year goes a-cold we know pine and cypress, then you can carve them.

XXVIII

1. He said: the wise are not flustered, the humane are not melancholy, the bold are not anxious.*

XXIX

1. He said: there are some we can study with, but cannot accompany in their mode of action; there are some we can collaborate with, but cannot build sound construction with, some we can construct with but not agree with as to the significance of what we are doing.

XXX

1. The flowers of the prunus japonica deflect and turn, do I not think of you dwelling afar?

2. He said: It is not the thought, how can there be distance in that?

BOOK TEN

Heang Tang
(*villeggiatura*)

I

1. Kung-tze in his village, looking as if he were too simple-hearted to utter.

2. In the dynastic temple, or court, speaking with easy pertinence; answering with prompt respect.

II

1. At court with the Lower-great officers straight from the shoulder; with the Upper-great officials with gentle courtesy.

---

*These are definitions of words.

233

2. With the sovran present, level alertness, grave readiness.

III

1. On the Prince calling him to receive a visitor, his face registered a change and his legs flexed.

2. He saluted (the officers whom he was standing with), left and right hand, his robe fore and aft evenly adjusted.

3. Swiftly advanced as if winged.

4. The visitor gone, it was his duty to report saying: the guest does not look back.

IV

1. Entering the ducal gate he hunched up like a ball as if there wasn't room.

2. Did not stand in the middle of the gateway, nor tread on the threshold-stone door-sill in going out.

3. Passing the sovran's standing place his expression changed and his legs seemed to flex, he spoke as if short of breath.

4. He went up the hall, he held his breath as if not breathing.

5. Coming out, when he had descended one step, his face relaxed to a pleasant expression, from the bottom of the steps he moved quickly, as if winged, to his place, still cagey on his feet.

V

1. Carrying the sceptre his body was bent as if it were too heavy to lift, the upper part at the level of the salute, the lower as when handing over something. His face grim, and his feet as if tethered.

2. Giving the ceremonial gifts, his face placid.

3. In private audience, as if enjoying it.

VI

1. Gentlemen do not (or the gentleman did not) wear dark purple puce ornaments.

2. Nor red purple in undress [*can also mean "mourning clothes"*].

3. Approximately in hot weather an unlined dress of linen or grass cloth must show and appear [L. over his underwear].

4. Black silk dress, lambskin; white dress fawn-skin; yellow dress fox fur.

5. Undress fur coat long with short sleeve [L. short right sleeve].

6. Had to have night gown half again as long as his body.

7. At home thick fox and badger fur.

8. Discarding mourning put all the gadgets on his belt.

9. Lower garments, except aprons, cut in (to the waist).

10. Lamb skin and black cap not used on visits of condolence.

11. At beginning of the month would always go to court in court dress.

VII

1. When fasting insisted on bright linen clothes.

2. For fasting had to change his diet, sit in a different place.

VIII

1. Couldn't get rice too clean or mince too fine for him.

2. Would not eat mouldy rice or fish or meat that had gone off, nor would he eat anything that had changed colour, stank, was ill cooked or out of season.

3. Did not eat meat badly cut or with the wrong sauce.

4. When there was a lot of meat he would not take more than what properly went with the rice, only in matter of wine was no blue nose (set no limit) but didn't get fuddled.

5. Did not take wine or eat dried meat from the market.

6. Always had ginger at table.

7. Didn't eat a great deal [or a lot of different things at a time?].

8. Did not keep the meat from the ducal sacrifices over night; nor that of the domestic sacrifice more than three days. It is not eaten after three days.

9. Did not talk while eating nor in bed.

10. Although but coarse rice or vegetable broth he would offer decorously a gourd (ladle-full) in sacrifice.

IX

1. Not sit on a mat askew.

X

1.   With villagers drinking, when the old fellows with canes went out, he followed.

2.   When the villagers drive out the devils in winter, he put on court robes and stood on his east steps.

XI

1.   On occasion of messengers from another state (or to it) he bowed twice and escorted the messenger out.

2.   Chi K'ang made him a present of medicine, he bowed and accepted it, saying: I don't know how far it goes, I don't dare take it.

XII

1.   The stable burned while he was away at court, he said: Any of the men hurt? not asking about the horses.

XIII

1.   On the prince sending food, he would adjust his mat and taste it before anyone else; the prince sending raw food he would cook it and set it before the spirits inviting them; if the prince sent him a live animal he would put it to pasture.

2.   In service of the prince at a feast, the prince sacrificed, first tasting.

> *Not clear, but L. evidently correct that Confucius acted as taster, either for prince, or for the spirits.*

3.   Being ill, the prince came to see him, he set his head to the east and had his court robes spread over him, his belt across them.

4.   When summoned by sovran order, he did not wait for the team to be hitched, he went on foot.

XIV

1.   Entering the great dynastic temple he asked about all details of the service.

XV

1.   When a friend died with no one to return (the body to its home for burial) he said: I will see to the funeral.

236

2. If a friend sent a present, though it were a carriage and pair, he did not bow, but only for a present of sacrificial meat.

XVI

1. In bed did not lie in the pose of a corpse; at home no formal manners.

2. Seeing anyone in mourning, although a familiar, he would change (his expression); seeing anyone in ceremonial cap, or blind, although he himself were in slops, he would salute with ceremony.

3. To a person in mourning he would bow over the dash-board. He would bow over the dash-board to anyone carrying the census tablets.

4. He would rise and bow with different expression at a feast with a loaded table.

5. He would change expression at sudden thunder or a keen gust of wind.

XVII

1. To get into the carriage he would stand plumb and take hold of the cord.

2. In the carriage he did not twist his head around, gabble, or point.

XVIII

1. "Beauty: That which arises, hovers, then comes to nest."

2. He said: Mountain ridge, the hen pheasant, the ringed pheasant the season, how! It is the season! Tze-lu [??] showed respect [3709 a ?], thrice smelled and rose. [? thrice inhaled the mountain air?]

> *Difficult as to the number of times the hen pheasant "hsiu" scented. Commentators in general give it up.*
>
> *P. apparently tries to connect the verse with the yellow bird that knows where to rest. Great Learning III, 2.*

BOOK ELEVEN

Hsien Tsin
The Earlier Approach

I

1. He said: Earlier approach to the rites and to music was the countryman's, the latter the gentleman's; I come at 'em the earlier way.

II

1. He said: None of those who followed me to Ch'an and Ts'ai now come to my door.

2. Showing *virtu* in act: Yen Yuan, Min Tze-ch'ien, Zan Po-niu, Chung-King; valued for their conversation: Tsai Wo, Tze-Kung; for administrative services: Zan Yu, Chi Lu; for their literary studies: Tze-yu, Tze-hsia.

III

1. He said: Hui's no help, he's pleased with everything I say.

IV

1. He said: Min Tze-ch'ien most certainly filial, no one disagrees with what his father, mother and all his brothers say (differs from what they say of him).

V

1. Nan Yung thrice came back to (quoting) "The White Sceptre"; Kung-tze gave him his elder brother's daughter to wife.

VI

1. Chi K'ang asked which of the disciples loved study. Kungtze answered: There was Yen Hui who loved study, unfortunately he died young, and the model's lost.

VII

1. Yen Yuan died and (his father) Yen Lu wanted Confucius to sell his carriage to pay for the coffin.

2. Confucius said: Talents or no talents every man calls his son, son. Li died and had a coffin but no outer shell. I did not

go on foot to get him an outer shell; having ranked just below the Great Officers, it was not fitting to go on foot.

VIII

1. Yen Yuan died, Confucius said: Heaven destroys me, destroys me.

IX

1. Yen Yuan died, and He mourned greatly; disciples said: This is excessive.
2. He said: Excessive?
3. If I do not greatly lament him, whom should I?

X

1. Yen Yuan died, the disciples wanted a big funeral. Confucius said: You may not.
2. The disciples gave a great funeral.
3. Confucius said: Hui treated me as a father. I have not managed to treat him as a son, not my fault but yours.

XI

1. Chi Lu asked about the service for ghosts and spirits. Confucius said: You cannot be useful to the living, how can you be useful to (serve) ghosts?
"Venture to ask about death."
Said: Not understanding life, how can you understand death? [Or "the living, how understand the dead?"]

XII

1. Min-tze was waiting on him looking respectful, Tze-Lu looking active, Zan Yu and Tze-Kung, frank and easy. He was pleased.
2. (Said): The Sprout, there, (Yu) won't die a natural death.

XIII

1. Lu folk in the matter of the new long Treasury building:
2. Min Tze-ch'ien said: What about repairing the old one? Why change and build?
3. He said: Great man for not talking, when he does it's mid target. [Chung, the middle, what it's all about.]

XIV

1. He said: What's Yu's lute doing at my door?

    [*Commentator's guess that "Sprout's" music was too warlike. Might distinguish "campaign" lute from scholar's lute? Must-lute and Now-lute.*]

2. The disciples did not revere Tzu-lu (Yu). He said: The Sprout has come up the hall, but not entered the inner apartment.

XV

1. Tze-Kung asked: Who's the better man, Shih or Shang? He said: Shih goes past the mark, Shang don't get there.

    (Tze-King) said: "So Shih's the better?"

    He said: It's as bad to overdo as not to get there.

XVI

1. The Chi chief was richer than the Duke of Chau, yet Ch'iu went on raking in taxes and piling up wealth for him.

2. Confucius said: No disciple of mine. The kids can beat drums and go after him (for all I care).

    "Taxes" is from Legge, Mathews follows it, but with no other illustration to back it up. (Lien [M. 3999] *is not among the different sorts of legalized tax mentioned by Mencius III.1, iii. 6. Han[4] (2052) must be a misprint in some editions.) Could be: went on raking it in, piling it up, supplementing his profits, his increase.*

XVII

1. Ch'ai is simple.
2. Shan is coarse.
3. Shih, deflected.
4. Yu ("the Sprout") is unkempt.

    All these adjectives unsatisfactory. Probably defined by the quality of the men described when they were used.

    It is assumed (by L. etc.) that they are pejorative. I cannot feel that the assumption is proved.

XVIII

1. He said: Hui's not far from it, frequently hard up. [K'ung *can mean also:* blank.]

2. Ts'ze does not receive (accept) destiny (? take orders) [L.: accept the decrees of Heaven], his riches fatten, his calculations are often correct.

1. Tze-Chang asked: How does a "shan⁴" man [*dictionary:* good man] act? He said: He does not trample footsteps [*note 502.7 combine, as "feelings"*], he does not enter the (inner) apartment.

> *This verse can only be taken as a definition of the word shan,⁴ which pictogrammically suggests symmetry, over a mouth. Goodness of the solar Ram, or what will you? L. takes it "inner chamber of the sage."*

XX

1. He said: Firm orderly discourse, we accept a fellow, but is he the real thing, or is it just gravity?*

XXI

1. Tze-Lu asked if he should act [L. immediately] on what he heard.

He said: Your father and elder brother are alive, why should you act on what you hear?

Zan Yu asked if he should act on what he heard. He said: When you hear it, do it.

Kung-hsi Hwa said: (Tze-Lu) Yu asked if he should act when he heard a thing, and you said: Your father and brother are alive. Ch'iu asked if he should act on what he heard, you said: Go to it. I am perplexed and venture. . . . Confucius said: Ch'iu is slow, therefore I prodded him; "the Sprout" too active, so I tried to slow him down.

XXII

1. He was in dread in Kwang, Yen Yuan came after him. He said: I thought you were dead.

(Yen) said: You are alive, how should I venture to die?

XXIII

1. Chi Tze-zan asked whether Chung Yu and Zan Ch'iu could be called great ministers.

2. He said: I thought you would ask about someone out of the ordinary, and you ask about Yu and Ch'iu.

3. You call a man a great minister when he serves his prince honestly, and retires when he cannot.

4. You can call Yu and Ch'iu "ministers" and that's all.

---

*Sterne: a mysterious carriage of the body, to conceal the defects of the mind. *Chuang*¹, sedateness, dressed-up-ness.

[*Or perhaps better "tool-ministers," 1556.b.*] *Pauthier with neat irony* "considerés comme ayant augmenté le nombre des ministres."

5. (Tze-zan) said: Aye, they'll always follow along.

6. He said: They would not follow along to parricide or regicide.

XXIV

1. Tze-Lu got Tze-Kao made governor of Pi.

2. He said: You are injuring somebody's son.

3. Tze-Lu said: There are men of the people, there are land altars and altars of the grain spirits, why do we need to read books and go on with study?

4. He said: That's why I hate big smart talk [fluency, L. glib-tongued people].

XXV

1. Tze-Lu, Tsang Hsi, Zan Yu, and Kung-hsi Hwa were sitting with him.

2. He said: I am a day older than you, but pay no attention to that.

3. You sit round saying: We are unknown, if somebody should recognize you, what would you do [L. like to do]?

4. Tze-Lu replied straight off the bat: "Thousand chariots' state. Shut in between large states, and armies of invasion, grain and provision famine, I could give the people courage if I had three years' run, and teach 'em the rules, put 'em on the square." The big man smiled (or grinned).

5. "Ch'iu, how about you?"

Replied: "Give me the job of a sixty, seventy or fifty li square district. I could give 'em abundant crops in three years. It would need a superior man to teach 'em the rites and music." ["*Abundant crops*"—*probably more literal*: there would be enough (for the) people.]

6. "What about you, Ch'ih?"

Replied: I don't say I could do that sort of thing, should like to study, serve in the ancestral temple, at audience of the princes, ceremonial chapter style [L. & M. dark square-made robe, black linen cap] to be lesser assistant.

7. "Chieh (clever-boy), what about you?" Struck his *se* (25-string lute) with curious jingling, laid down the lute and

got up, answering: Differ from the three of 'em in what they grasp at.

Confucius said: What harm, let each say what he wants (*directio voluntatis*).

(Chieh) said: Toward the end of spring, in nice spring clothes, with five or six fellows who have been capped, and six or seven kids, go bathe in I river (Shantung) with the wind over the rain dance [*probably*, wind for the rain dance, *could be*: wind suitable for the rain dance] to chant (through the service) and go home.

The big man heaved a sigh of assent: I am with Chieh.

> [*L. calls this young man Tien.*]

8. The three went out, Tsang Hsi delaying, and said: What about these three men's words? Confucius said: Each one expressed his preference, that's all.

9. (Hsi) said: Boss, why did you grin at "The Sprout"?

10. He said: A state is managed with ceremony, his words were not polite, so I grinned.

11. "But Ch'iu didn't ask for a state."

"Calmly, did you ever see a district fifty, sixty or seventy li square that wasn't a state?"

12. "Only Ch'ih, was he asking for a state?"

"Together in ancestral temple, who save nobles would be there; if Ch'ih were a lesser acolyte, who'd be the big ones?"

BOOK TWELVE

I

1. Yen Yuan asked about full manhood. He said: Support oneself and return to the rites, that makes a man.

> [*The "support oneself" is fairly literal. It cannot be limited to superficial idea of making a living, but certainly need not be taken ascetically. "Determine the character" might render one side of the phrase.*]

If a man can be adequate to himself for one day and return to the rites, the empire would come home to its manhood. This business of manhood sprouts from oneself, how can it sprout from others?

2. Yen Yuan said: Wish I had the eye to see it, may I ask?

If something is contrary to the rites, don't look at it; don't listen to it, don't discuss it, if it is contrary to the rites don't spend energy on it. Yen Yuan said: I am not clever but I would like to act on that advice.

II

1. Chung-kung asked about full manhood. He said: Out of doors look on men as if you were receiving great guests; put men to work as if you were performing the Great Sacrifice, what you don't want (done to you) don't do to another, settle in a district without fault-finding, take root in the home without fault-finding.

Chung-kung said: I'm not clever, but I'd like to put those words into practice.

III

1. Sze-ma Niu asked about manhood. He said: The full man's words have an edge of definition. [*L. merely:* slow of speech.]

2. (Niu) said: [*as L.*] Cautious and slow of speech, is that a definition of manhood? He said: Difficult business to reach one's verbal manifest in one's actions unless the words are defined [*L.:* unless the speech be slow].

[*The right hand component of this* jen[4] *is clearly shaped as* jen (4) 3110; *not as in M.'s* 3117, *but not in all printed editions.*]

IV

1. Sze-ma Niu asked about (the term) gentleman. He said: The man of breed has neither melancholy nor fears.

2. (Niu) said: Being without retrospective melancholy or fear, is that being the gentleman? [*Or:* How does that constitute the *chun tzu?*]

3. He said: On introspection nothing wrong (diseased), how would he have regrets or fears?

V

1. Sze-ma Niu said in worry (or regret): Everyone has brothers except me. I haven't (or have lost 'em).

2. Tze-Hsia said: "I've heard said:

3. "Death and life have their sealed orders, riches and honours are from heaven."

4. The man with the voices of his forebears within him is reverent; he gives men respect, and holds to the right usage, all men within the four seas are elder and younger brothers. How can the proper man be distressed for lack of brothers?

VI

1. Tze-chang asked about light. He said: He whom slow soaking slander, and

> tiger-stomach receive inform

[*L. "statements that startle"*]

> have no effect on (are no go with) can be called enlightened [*bis* can be called perspicuous, far-seeing].

VII

1. Tze-Kung asked about government. He said: Enough food, enough weapons, and that the people stand by their word [L. have confidence in their ruler].

2. Tze-Kung said: If you can't manage this, which do you omit first? He said: The armaments.

3. Tze-Kung: If you can't manage the other two, which do you omit first? He said: The food. All must die, but if the people be without faith (fail of their word) nothing stands.

VIII

1. Chi Tze-ch'ang said: A proper man needs the solid qualities, that's enough, what's the use of higher culture?

2. Tze-kung said: Pity the great philosopher's words, he is a superior man (but) four horses cannot overtake the tongue.

3. The finish is as the substance, the solid, the substance like the polish it takes; tiger-skin, leopard-skin are like dog-skin and goat-skin if you take the hair off.

IX

1. The Duke Ai said to Yu Zo: Bad year, scant harvest, what's to be done?

2. Yu Zo: Why not tithe?

3. "Two tenths not enough, how would I manage with one?"

4. Answered: If the hundred clans have enough, who won't give enough to the prince, if the hundred clans are in want who will give enough to the prince?

> *The great discussion of the tenth tithe vs/fixed charge, is given in Mencius* III.1. iii, 6.

X

1. Tze-chang asked about raising the level of conscience and detecting illusions (delusions). He said: The first thing is: get

245

to the centre (what it is all "about"), stand by your word, respect the meum and tuum, that will elevate your virtue (level of conscious acts).

2. Love a man, you wish he may live; hate and you wish him to die; then you wish him to live, and turn round and want him to die, that is a muddle.

3. "Really it is not on account of the wealth, and yet you note a difference." [*This refers to Odes* II, IV, 4, 3, *the brother of the first wife, taking leave of brother-in-law remarried to a rich woman.*]

XI

1. Duke Ching of Ch'i asked Kung-tze about government.

2. Kung-tze replied: Prince to be prince; minister, minister; father, father; son, son.

3. The Duke said: Good. I stand by that, if the prince be not prince; minister not minister; father not father; son not son, although there is grain can I manage to eat it all?

> L. "*Although I have my revenue, can I enjoy it?*" *Possibly:* "*although there is grain will I have time to eat it?*" *M. gives no example of* chu (1) *interrogative.*

XII

1. He said: Settle disputes with half a word, "the Sprout" could do that.

2. Tze-lu (the Sprout) never slept on a promise.

XIII

1. He said: In hearing litigations I am like another, the thing is to have no litigation, *n'est-ce pas?*

XIV

1. Tze-chang asked about government. He said: Not to lie down on it; to act from the middle of the heart.

XV

1. He said: Extensive study for accomplishments; restraint by the rites; by short-cuts across fields you lose the great road.

XVI

1. He said: The proper man brings men's excellence to focus, he does not focus their evil qualities; the mean man does the reverse.

XVII

1. Chi K'ang asked Confucius about government. Kung-tze replied: Government consists in correcting; if you lead by being correct, who will dare be incorrect?

XVII

1. Chi K'ang worried about thieves, questioned Confucius. Kung-tze answered: If you weren't covetous, they wouldn't steal even if you paid 'em.

XIX

1. Chi K'ang asked Confucius about government: "What about killing the wayward for the benefit of the well behaved?"

Kung-tze answered: Why kill to govern? If you want the good, the people will be good; the proper man acting according to his conscience is wind, the lesser folk acting on conscience, grass; grass with wind above it must bend.

XX

1. Tze-chang asked what an officer should be like to go far.

2. He said: What do you call going far?

3. Tze-chang said: To be heard of throughout the state, to be heard of in his clan.

4. He said: That's notoriety not distinction (or perspicacity, making a wide noise not getting very far).

5. The far-effective man is solid, upright, loves justice; examines peoples' words, looks into their faces, thinks how, in what way, he is inferior to them, roots in the state and goes far; roots in his family and effects things at a distance.

6. The notorious bloke puts up a show of manhood, and acts counter to it, perfectly confident; is heard about to the end of the state, makes a noise throughout all his clan.

XXI

1. Fan Ch'ih walking with him below the rain altars (or to celebration of the rain sacrifice pantomime) said: Venture to ask how to lift one's conscience in action; to correct the hidden tare, and separate one's errors?

2. He said: An excellent question!

3. Put first the action, second the success. Won't that raise the level of your conscious acts? Work on one's own faults, not on someone else's hatefulnesses, won't that comb out the hidden weeds?

For one morning's temper to jeopard one's life and even that of one's relatives, isn't that hallucination?

XXII

1. Fan Ch'ih asked about humaneness. He said: Love men. Asked about knowledge. He said: To know men.

2. Fan Ch'ih didn't get as far (see through to the end of that answer).

3. He said: Promote the straight, and grind the crooked, that way you can straighten 'em.

4. Fan Ch'ih retired, and seeing Tze-Hsia said: Just saw the big man and asked him about knowledge. He said: Promote the straight and grind the crooked, that way you can straighten the crooks, how did he mean it?

5. Tze-Hsia said: That's a rich and ample saying.

6. Shun had the Empire, picked out Kao-Yao from the multitude, promoted him, and wrong 'uns departed. T'ang had the Empire, he picked out I Yin from all the hordes, promoted him, and the wrong 'uns departed.

XXIII

1. Tze-Kung asked about friendship. He said: Speak out from the centre of your mind, maintain the true process, if he can't hitch to it, don't disgrace yourself.

XXIV

1. Tsang-tze said: The proper man makes friends on the basis of culture, and by his friends develops his manhood (or develops his manhood through this fluid exchange).

BOOK THIRTEEN

Tze-Lu, the Sprout

I

1. Tze-Lu asked about government. He said: Go ahead, and work at it.

2. Asked further. Said: Don't lie down on it.

II

1. Chung-kung being minister of the Chi Head asked about government. He said: First get your assistants, overlook small faults and promote men of solid talent.

248

2. Said: How shall I know men of solid talent?

Said: Promote those you do know, will everybody then neglect those whom you don't?

III

1. Tze-Lu said: The Lord of Wei is waiting for you to form a government, what are you going to do first?

2. He said: Settle the names (determine a precise terminology).

3. Tze-lu said: How's this, you're divagating, why fix 'em?

4. He said: You bumpkin! Sprout! When a proper man don't know a thing, he shows some reserve.

5. If words (terminology) are not (is not) precise, they cannot be followed out, or completed in action according to specifications.

6. When the services (actions) are not brought to true focus, the ceremonies and music will not prosper; where rites and music do not flourish punishments will be misapplied, not make bullseye, and the people won't know how to move hand or foot (what to lay hand on, or stand on).

7. Therefore the proper man must have terms that can be spoken, and when uttered be carried into effect; the proper man's words must cohere to things, correspond to them (exactly) and no more fuss about it.

IV

1. Fan Ch'ih asked to be taught agriculture. He said: I am not as good as an old peasant. Asked to study gardening. He said: I am not as good as an old gardener.

2. Fan Ch'ih went out. He said: What a nit-wit, that Fan.

3. If the men above love the rites no one of the people will dare be irreverent. If the men above love justice, none of the people will fail to conform, if the men above love veracity, none of the people will want to use mendacity, when the Great one is like this, the people of the Four Squares will come to him with their children on their backs, what does he need to know about farming?

V

1. Reciting the three hundred odes, given a government mission and not understanding it, sent to the Four Coigns and not being able to give the answers, even with a lot of talk won't be

able to carry it through. [L.: notwithstanding extent of his learning, what practical use is it?]

VI

1. He said: When a prince's character is properly formed, he governs without giving orders (without orders, things go on). If his character is twisty he can give orders, but they won't be carried out.

VII

1. He said: The governments (forms of government) of Lu and Wei: elder and younger brothers.

VIII

1. He described Ching, a younger member of the Ducal family in Wei, by saying: He knew how to live (run a house). When he began to own something he said: what a lot. When he had a bit more, he said: this is enough. When rich, he said: how magnificent.

IX

1. When he went to Wei, Zan Yu drove.
2. He said: What's the population?
3. Zan Yu said: Well populated, what next? Said: Enrich them.
4. Said: They are rich, what next? Said: Educate.

X

1. He said: If anybody had used me for twelve months I'd have been able to do something, and in three years to have done something perfect.

XI

1. He said: Honest men govern a country a hundred years, they could vanquish the malevolent and get rid of the death penalty. I mean these precise words.
   [*Possibly the first time anyone had thought of this.*]

XII

1. He said: With a real king, it would need a generation to produce the consequent humanization.

XIII

1. He said: If a man correct himself what difficulty will he have in consequent government, if he cannot correct himself,

what's he doing in (or with) government, anyhow? [P. *comment pourrait-il rectifier la conduite des autres?*]

XIV

1.   To Zan-tze, coming from court, he said: Why so late? Answered: There was official business.   He said: May have been business *affaires du prince,* but if it were government business, even though I'm not in office, been very hard for me not to hear of it.

XV

1.   Duke Ting asked if there were one sentence that could bring prosperity to a state.   Kung-tze answered: One sentence could hardly put all that in motion.

[*cf*/Great Learning, Mature Study IX.3, *semina motuum.*]

2.   There is a saying: it is difficult to be a prince, not easy to be a minister.

3.   Knowing it is difficult to be prince, this one sentence might nearly bring prosperity to a state.

4.   Said: Is there one sentence that can ruin a state?   Kung-tze answered: Hardly, but there's a saying: no pleasure in being prince save that no one can go counter to what I say.

5.   If good and unopposed that's all right?   But if evil and no one oppose, that's almost enough to ruin a state? *N'est-ce pas?*

XVI

1.   The Duke of Sheh asked about government.

2.   He said: Those near, happy; those afar, attracted and come.

XVII

1.   Tze-Hsia, being governor of Chu-fu, asked about government.   He said: Not want things rushed, and not on the lookout for small profits; if you want things rushed they won't go through to the end;* looking for small profits, the big jobs won't be done right.

XVIII

1.   The Duke of Sheh said to Kung-tze: There are honest characters in my village, if a man steals a sheep his son will bear witness to it.

2.   Kung-tze said: There are honest men in my village with this difference; a father will conceal his son's doing, and a son his father's.   There's honesty (straight seeing) in that, too.

*P. *Alors vous ne les comprendrez bien.*

251

XIX

1. Fan Ch'ih asked about full manhood. He said: When living in comfort to be modest, when taking hold of affairs to observe honest procedure.

> *If one is to distinguish the* kung[1] *from the* ching[4] *I think we must take it as between stasis and kinesis, the* ching *containing the radical for beat, and going back, I take it, to beating on the earth to propitiate the grain spirits (grass on top left, and various meanings of the* chü *(1541, a, b)—both terms given in dictionary as reverent).*

With sincerity in what you give men, even among the wild tribes (bowmen, and with dogs at camp-fire) east and north, these qualities cannot be shed (cannot be wasted, *leaf fallen, from tree rad/*).

XX

1. Tze-kung asked for the definition of an officer. He said: He has a sense of shame, if you send him to the last corner of the realm, he will carry out the prince's decrees and not disgrace himself.

2. Said: What's the next thing to that? [*Or as L.*: What category next?] Said: His own temple group weigh him and find him filial, folk in his own village knowing his weight find him brotherly.

3. Said: May I ask what next? Said: When he speaks he must stick to his word; acts must be consequent, water-on-stone, water-on-stone (persistent) little men, mebbe they constitute the next lot.

4. Said: What about the lot now in government? He said: Pint-pots and bamboo baskets (or buckets, utensils), count 'em as that, it'll do. [*E poi basta.*] (*Aliter*: they can use an abacus, calculate their own advantage, *or simply "all told".*)

XXI

1. He said: Not being able give to (be with) men who act on "what it is all about," I must (teach) the pushing and the cautious; the forward will go ahead and take hold; the cautious will stick to not doing what's not to be done. [*P. s'abstiennent au moins de pratiquer ce qui dépasse leur raison.*]

XXII

1. He said: The people of the South have a saying: an unconstant (inconsistent, inconsequent) man can't rise to be a wizard

or doctor (better: can neither invoke nor cure), that's a good one.

2. Inconsistent (incoherent) in carrying his inwit into act, likely to meet disgrace.

3. He said: Not observing the signs, and that's all.

[? *a simple inattention enough to bring his downfall or:* he does not observe the signs, and that's all there is to be said about it; *for the doctor it would be symptoms, fails to diagnose, thus defining the word* heng², *consequent;* pu heng, *not consequent. One must insist on the nature of many verses as being set down in order to define particular words, as did Lorenzo Valla in his Elegantiae. Also Kung's laconism, highly pleasing to some readers.*]

XXIII

1. He said: The proper man is pleasant spoken but not just like everyone else. The small man is identical but not agreeable.

XXIV

1. Tze-kung said: What about a fellow that everyone in the village likes? He said: Won't do.

"What about a fellow everyone in his village hates?" He said: Won't do. Not up to the man whom the decent people in the village like and the wrong 'uns hate.

XXV

1. He said: The superior man is easy to serve and hard to please. Try to please him with something crooked and he won't be pleased. He employs men in accordance with their capacity. The mean man is easy to please and hard to work for. You can please him by doing wrong. He wants to get everything out of the same man.

XXVI

1. He said: The proper man is liberal and not high-horsey [*The* t'ai⁴. 6023 *liberal, hand grip over water rad/can also mean exalted, with the cross-light, lofty, high-minded and not proud*] (honoured and not proud). The mean man is proud and not high-minded (honoured, honourable).

XXVII

1. He said: The firm-edge, the persistent, the tree-like, those who hold in their speech, come near to full manhood.

No, *reticent. And to combat anyone who thinks Karlgren a mere academic, cf/his note on "the impure light of fire that shines outward, the pure light of water that shines inward."*

XXVIII

1. Tze-lu said: What's the real definition of a scholar. He said: Urgent, quiet; [M. *gives the three terms:* earnest, pressing, pleased] standing by or looking at his own thought, his own mind-field or heart-field, easy to get on with (i^2) cheerful. [*I shd/ be inclined to add "spontaneous" to possible meanings of this* i^2.] He can be called a scholar (-officer), earnest with his friends, and stimulating; cheerful and spontaneous with his elder and younger brothers.

XXIX.

1. If a good man teach the people for seven years, they can go to war.

XXX

1. He said: To send an untrained people to war is to throw them away.

BOOK FOURTEEN

Hsien Wan
Hsien asked

I

1. Hsien asked what is shameful. He said: When the country has a good government to be thinking only of salary; when the country has bad government, to be thinking only of salary: that is shameful.

II

1. "When the letch to get on, to make a show, when resentments and greeds aren't given way to; that makes manhood?"

2. He said: That constitutes doing what's difficult. As to its being full manhood *(humanitas)*, I don't know.

III

1. He said: Loving comfort, cuddling domesticity, is not enough to make a scholar (scholar-officer, *shih*).

IV

1. He said: When the country is decently governed: daring

words; daring acts. When the country is not decently governed, daring acts and conventional speech. [Sun *in first tone, a grandson; in 4th: Prudent, docile, reserved.*]

V

1. He said: He who has the *virtu* to act on his inwit must have words, but he who has words needn't necessarily act according to conscience. He who is manly must have courage, audacity, but he who is audacious needn't necessarily have full *humanitas*, manhood.

VI

1. Nan-kung Kuo said to Kung-tze: Yi was a good archer, Ao could drag a boat along on land, neither died a natural death. Yu and Chi did their own farm-work and rose to be emperors. The big man didn't reply. Nan-kung Kuo went out. He said: A proper man, that! what a man ought to be like. Respects conscientious action as a man should.

VII

1. He said: Superior men aren't always complete; no mean man has manhood.
> *The language is very close; one might say,* a man can have the voice of his ancestry within him, without attaining complete *humanitas*. No mean man has *humanitas*.

VIII

1. He said: Love exists, can it be other than exigent? Where there is sincerity (mid-mind, mid-heart) can it refrain from teaching?
> [*"word-each."* 2338. hui[4]. *Again it is instruction by sorting out terms. Can you get the centre of the mind, without terminology?*]

IX

1. He said: Drawing up the decrees (government orders) P'i Shan invented the straw (i.e., made the rough drafts), Shih-shu inched the words* and discussed them with the Chef du Protocole (the *Hsing jen*, official in charge of travelling envoys), Tze-Yu combed 'em out and polished 'em, and Tze-Chan of Tung Li added the beauties.

---

*P. (?) *les examinait attentivement et y plaçait les dits des anciens.*

1. Someone asked about (this) Tze-Chan. He said: A kind man.

2. Asked about Tze-Hsi. He said: That bloke! That one! [*If you accept Legge's interpretation, but the* pi tsai *might be perhaps taken as: "just another,* uomo qualunque." *There just isn't enough in the text to indicate tone of voice: query, alas? or what will you!*]

3. Asked about Kwan Chung. He said: *Jen yeh**, man who snatched from Po chief, P'ien, a city of three hundred (L. families), (L. the latter) ate coarse rice till his teeth were gone (L. and current, till death) without a grumbling word. [*L.'s note, that the dispossessed respected Kwan to this extent.*]

XI

1. He said: To be poor without grumbling or resentments is difficult; easy to be rich and not haughty.

XII

1. He said: Mang Kung-ch'o for being an elder (senex, senator) of the Chao or Wei, has it in abundance (easily more than fill the pattern requirements), couldn't make it as Great Officer of Tang or Hsieh.

XIII

1. Tze-Lu asked about the perfect man (the man of perfect focus).

He said: As if he had Tsang Wu-chung's knowledge, Kung-ch'o's freedom from greed, Chwang of Pien's bravery, Zan Ch'iu's versatile talents, culture enough for the rites and music, he'd have the wherewithal for human perfection.

2. Said: At present why need we such perfect humanity; to see chance of profit and consider equity, to see danger and be ready to accept one's fate, not to forget the level words of a compact made long ago, that also would make a focus'd man (a man brought to the point, perfect).

XIV

1. Asking about Kung shu Wan, he said to Kung-ming Chia: Do you stick by the statement that your big man doesn't talk, doesn't smile, doesn't accept anything?

---

*Possibly wider reading wd/ enlighten as to bearing of Chinese equivalents of, Oh, ugh, and ah! and any flavour that might have been kept in a strictly oral tradition as to tone of voice used. Here it seems to be approbative, and the *tsai* seems pejorative in verse 2.

2. Kung-ming Chia replied: That's from rumours (reports) overrunning the limit. My big man talks when it's the time, whereby he does not bore with his talking; smiles when pleased, thereby not boring with grins; when it is just to take, he accepts, thus he don't wear people out with taking. He said: Yes, does he really do that?

XV

1. He said: Tsang Wu-chung flowing thru Fang, asked Lu to appoint a successor; although you say this is not bringing pressure to bear on a prince, I won't stand by that definition.

XVI

1. He said: Duke Wan of Tsin was wily and not correct, [chüeh²⁻⁵; wily *from words and an awl, clouds of three colours, hypocrite. P. admirably:* un fourbe sans droiture.]
Duke Hwan of Ch'i was correct and not wily.

XVII

1. Tze-lu said: Duke Hwan executed the Ducal-son (his brother) Chiu; Shao Hu died [L. with his boss], Kwang Chung did not die, say, is that inhumane (unmanly?)?

2. He said: Duke Hwan gathered the princes, not with weapons and war cars: Kwan Chung's energy (strength) that was; is that manly? It is manly.

XVIII

1. Tze-Kung [*not to be confused with Kung (fu) tze*] said: I'd give it that Kwan Chung was lacking in humanity, Duke Hwan had his brother Chiu bumped off, and (Kwan Chung) couldn't die, but came back and worked with Hwan as (Prime Minister).

2. He said: Kwan Chung reciprocal'd, aided Duke Hwan as prime minister, overruling the princes; unified and rectified the empire, and people till today receive the benefits. But for Kwan Chung we'd be wearing our hair loose and buttoning our coats to the left.

3. You want him to behave like a common man or woman, who could end in a creek or ditch without anyone's being the wiser?

XIX

1. Kung-shu Wan's minister, the Great Officer Hsien, rose shoulder to shoulder with Wan in this Duke's (court).

2. Confucius hearing this said: Wan's the name for him [*Wan*, accomplished, having real culture] on that count.

XX

1. He was speaking of the evil government of the Duke Ling of Wei (Nan-tze's husband). K'ang-tze said: A man like that, how come he don't lose (his state)?

2. Kung-tze said: The second brother Yu looks after guests and strangers; the ecclesiastic T'o looks after the dynastic temple; Wang-sun Chia looks after the army corps and regiments, men like that, how lose his (state)?

XXI

1. He said: If a man don't say what he means, it's difficult to shape business to it, action to it. [*L. and M. take the* put se *as meaning immodest. Pictogrammic interpretation at least as interesting.*]

XXII

1. Chan Ch'ang murdered the Duke of Ch'i.

2. Confucius took a bath, went to court, and made formal announcement to the Duke Ai, in these words: Chan Ch'ang has murdered his prince; this invites punishment.

3. The Duke said: Inform the Three Great.

4. Kung-tze said: Coming (in rank) just after the Great Officers, I did not venture to leave my prince uninformed. (My prince) says inform the Three Great.

5. He announced it to the Three, (who pled) *non possumus.* Kung-tze said: Coming just after the Great Officers, I did not dare omit the announcement.

XXIII

1. Tze-lu asked about serving a prince. He said: Don't cheat him, stand up to him [L. withstand him to his face].

XXIV

1. He said: A proper man progresses upward (far), a mean man progresses downward (far).

> *Might almost say:* goes far up, far down. All the way through, penetrates upward or downward. *Covers the meaning:* his mental penetration goes upward, or downward.

XXV

1. He said: In the old days men studied to make themselves, now they study to impress others.

XXVI

1. Chu Po-yu sent a man to Confucius.

2. Kung-tze sat with him and questioned him: What's your boss doing?

Replied: "My big man wants to diminish the number of his errors, and cannot." The messenger went out. Kung-tze said: Some messenger, isn't he?

XXVII

1. He said: Not in a particular government office, don't plan to run it.

XXVIII

1. Tsang-tze (his son-in-law) said: A proper man's thoughts do not go outside (the sphere of) his office. [Yi King *diagram 52, eight characters, here seven, omitting one.*]

XXIX

1. He said: A proper man is ashamed of words [L. modest in speech], and goes beyond (them) in action. [*Also:* ashamed of words that exceed his action.]

XXX

1. He said: A proper man's mode of life is three-ply. I can't make it: manhood without regrets; knowing, he is without suspicion; courageous and therefore without anxiety.

2. Tze-Kung said: Boss, that's the way you go on yourself.

XXXI

1. Tze-Kung square-measured men (one by another). Confucius said: Tze, you must have heavy talents, *n'est-ce pas?* Anyhow, I haven't got the spare time.

XXXII

1. He said: Not worried that others don't know me, worried by my incapacities.

XXXIII

1. He said: Not anticipating deceit or calculating on infidelity [L. anticipate attempts to deceive him, nor think beforehand of not being believed. *Might even be:* don't oppose deceit (to de-

ceit) or calculate on a man's lies, or lying], but to be quick to spot a hoax when it happens, man who can do this must have solid sense?

XXXIV

1. In course of conversation (old) Wei-shang Mau, said to him: Hummock, my boy, how do you manage to roost when there's a roost going, do you manage it by an oily tongue?

2. He said: I don't dare oil the tongue, but I hate stick-in-a-rut-ness (hate being boxed in with frowst).

XXXV

1. He said: A horse is grade A not because of strength but from a balance of qualities (proportionate ensemble).

> *This is another definition, directing thought to the composition of the ideogram itself. A "separate differences horse," extraordinary, yes, defined by the* ch'eng, *with sense of weighing of the grain, good grain, agreeable etc.* (383) vid. *also alternations* (3067).

XXXVI

1. Someone said what about returning straight goodness for injury [L. kindness for injury]?

2. He said: What do you do to repay someone who acts straight with you?

3. See straight when someone injures you, and return good deeds by good deeds.

> *L. has the old:* justice for injury, kindness for kindness. *This does not exhaust the contents of the ideograms.* Yüan (4th): *murmur, harbour resentment. Allay resentment by straightness, watch a man who harbours resentment against you. Give frank act for frank act. Understanding of Confucius has been retarded by wanting to fit his thought into gross occidental cliches.*

XXXVII

1. He said: The extent to which no one understands me!

2. Tze-kung said: How do you make out no one understands you (knows you)?

He said: I do not harbour resentment against heaven, I study what is below and my thought goes on, penetrates upward. Is it heaven that knows me? [*Not id. but cf/Aristotle: generals* FROM *particulars.*]

XXXVIII

1. Kung-po Liao slandered [*currently "smeared"*] Tze-Lu to Chi-sun [*cd. be:* definitely brought formal charge against him, *or:* laid an information, pejorative, or definitely false]. Tze-fu Ching-po told of it, saying: The big man is certainly having his intentions misled (direction of his will deflected) by Kung-po Liao, I have strength enough to have him executed in the market place or in court. [*i. e. as common criminal or great officer*].

2. He said: If my mode of living is to make headway, or if my process is to go to waste, it is destined [*seal and mouth of heaven*]; what can Kung-po Liao do about that decree?

XXXIX

1. He said: Some with solid talents get away from their generation.

2. Those nearest (that solidity) retire from a particular locality.

3. The next grade get away from dazzle (display).

4. Those next get away from words [the dominion of catch phrases. *Cd/ even be:* stop talking].

> 5172, *in various connotations.* (i): *look down upon. rad/ 160. "bitter". A cross under rad/ 117. looks not unlike a graph of a spinning-whorl.*

XL

1. He said: Seven men started this [L. have done this].

XLI

1. Tze-lu was passing the night at Stone Gate, the gate guard said: Where from?

Tze-lu said: The Kung clan.

Said: He's the man who knows there's nothing to be done, yet sticks with it (keeps on trying).

XLII

1. He was drumming on the musical stone in Wei, a man with a straw hamper on his back passed the door of the Kung family house, and said: What a mind he's got beating that stone, *n'est ce pas?*

2. That was that, then he said: How vulgar! Persistent,

water on stone, water on stone. When one is not recognized that's the end of it, end it. "Over deep with your clothes on, pick 'em up when the water is shallow." (Odes I. iii. 9.)

3. He said: Certainly, no difficulty about that.

[*The text does not give one sufficient to insist on the bearing of the* kuo, 3732, *fruit.*]

XLIII

1. In the History, Tze-chang said: What's the meaning of the statement: Kao-tsung observing the imperial mourning did not speak for three years?

2. He said: Why drag in Kao-tsung, in the old days everyone did. When the sovereign died, the hundred officers carried on, getting instructions from the prime minister for three years.

XLIV

1. He said: When men high up love the rites the people are easily governed.

XLV

1. Tze-lu asked about "right 'uns." He said: (The proper man) disciplines himself with reverence for the forces of vegetation.

Said: Is that all there is to it?

Said: Disciplines himself and quiets others (rests them, considers their quiet).

Said: Disciplines himself and brings tranquillity to the hundred clans. Discipline self and quiet the hundred clans, Yao and Shun were almost in agony over that (almost painfully anxious to do that).

XLVI

1. Yuan Zang remained squatting on his heels as Kung approached.

He said: Young and not deferentially (holding the line) fraternal, come to manhood and not transmitting, old and not dying, exactly a burglarious bum. Hit him over the shin with his cane.

XLVII

1. A young Ch'ueh villager ran errands for him, someone said: Up and coming?

2. He said: I see him sit in men's chairs, walk abreast of his elders, he's not trying to fill up, he's trying to finish in a hurry.

BOOK FIFTEEN

Wei Ling Kung
Duke Ling of Wei

I

1. Duke Ling of Wei asked Kung-tze about tactics. Kung-tze replied: I have heard a bit about sacrificial stands and dishes, I have not studied the matter of army arrangements. He left next morning.

2. In Chan, provisions cut off, those following him sickened so no one could get up.

3. Tze-Lu showing his irritation said: Does a gentleman have to put up with this sort of thing? He said: A gentleman gets obstinate when he has to; a small man dissolves (when he's up against it).

II

1. He said: Tz'u ("Grant"), you think I make a lot of studies and commit things to memory?

Replied: Aye, ain't it so?

Said: No, I one, through, string-together, sprout [*that is*: unite, flow through, connect, put forth leaf]. For me there is one thing that flows through, holds things together, germinates.

III

1. He said: Sprout, few know how to carry their inwit straight into acts.

IV

1. He said: Shun governed without working. How did he do it? He soberly corrected himself and sat looking to the south (the sovereign sat on a throne looking south), that's all.

V

1. Tze-chang asked about conduct.

2. He said: Speak from the plumb centre of your mind, and keep your word; bamboo-horse your acts [*that is*, have this quality of surface hardness, and suppleness] with reverence for the vegetative powers, even if you are among the wild men of the South and North (Man and Mo), that is the way to act. If you speak without this candour, and break your word; if you act without polish (honour) and reverence, how will it go even in your own bailiwick (department [*and*] neighbourhood)?

3.   Standing (stablishing, building up a heap) let him form a triad looking at those two powers before him (*either* facing him, *or* existing there before him).

>   *Note the three "armstrongs," bent arms with biceps, in upper part of the* ts'an *ideogram, and use of same in* The Pivot XXII, *last line.*

In his carriage let him see them hitched to the yoke [*from rad 144, as traces or reins. Contrast: "like a carriage with no place to hitch the traces"*], then he can proceed.

4.   Tze-chang wrote these (words) on his belt.

VI

1.   He said: Straight, and how! the historian Yu. Country properly governed, he was like an arrow; country in chaos he was like an arrow.

2.   Some gentleman, Chu Po-yu! country decently governed, he is in office; when the government is rotten he rolls up and keeps the true process inside him.

VII

1.   He said: When you can talk to a man, and don't, you lose the man; when it's no use talking to a man, and you talk to him, you waste words. An intelligent man wastes (loses) neither men nor words.

VIII

1.   He said: An officer (scholar) ruling his mind, a humane man (man of full manhood) will not try to live by damaging his manhood; he will even die to perfect his humanitas.

>   *There are probably earlier expressions of this concept; I have not yet found an earlier statement as to abolition of the death penalty.* Vide supra XIII, xi.

IX

1.   Tze-kung asked about this business of manhood. He said: The craftsman wanting to perfect his craft must first put an edge on his tools (take advantage of implements already there, the containers). Living in a country, take service with the big men who have solid merit, make friends with the humane scholar-officers.

X

1.   Yen Yuan asked about governing.

2.   He said: Go along with the seasons of Hsia [*the Hsia*

calendar, but probably including the dates for the markets, however computed].

3. *L. & M. both say:* Use Yin state carriages. [*I think it may refer to the gauge, the wheel-spread, cf/ ref/ to uniform gauge of wheel-ruts.*]

4. Wear the Chou coronation cap [*mortar board with fringe. I suppose this is related to four-squareness, Urzahl*].

5. Music patterned to the Shao pantomimes.

6. Banish the ear-noise* of Chang, and clear out the flatterers. The tonalities of Chang are slushy, and double-talkers a danger (diddling, debauching).

XI

1. He said: Man who don't think of the far, will have trouble near.

XII

1. He said: Can't get beyond the fact; I have not seen anyone who loves acting from inwit as they love a beautiful person.

XIII

1. He said: Tsang Wan-chung like a man who has purloined his position, he knew the solid merit of Hui of Lin-hsia, and did not get him for colleague.

XIV

1. He said: Requiring the solid from himself and the trifling from others, will keep one far from resentments.

XV

1. He said: When a man don't say, "What's it like, what's it like?" I don't (bother to) compare him to anything, and that's that (*aliter:* I don't know where he'll end up).

XVI

1. He said: Gabbling all day without getting to a discussion of equity (ethics, justice), in love with being clever in a small way; hard to do anything with 'em.

XVII

1. He said: The proper man gives substance (makes the substance of his acts equity) to his acts by equity.

---

* P. (excellently): *modulations.*

Cf/ *final words of the* Ta S'eu: The treasure of a state is its equity, *or, better, as all Confucian statements treat of process not stasis:* What profits a state is its honesty.

He proceeds according to the rites, puts them forth modestly, and makes them perfect by sticking to his word. That's the proper man (in whom's the voice of his forebears).

XVIII

1. He said: The proper man is irritated by his incapacities, not irritated by other people not recognizing him.

XIX

1. He said: The gentleman is irritated if his generation die without weighing the worth of his name.

This sentence illustrates the inadequacy of "gent" as in current parlance of the last century, to translate chun tzu. cf/ Dial *essay 25 years ago. L. gives:* name not mentioned after his death. *v. weak for ch'eng 383. from grain rad/*

XX

1. The proper man seeks everything in himself, the small man tries to get everything from somebody else.

XXI

1. He said: The proper man is punctilious but not quarrelsome, he is for exchange, not provincial.

XXII

1. He said: The proper man does not promote a fellow for what he says; nor does he throw out a statement because of who says it.

XXIII

1. Tze-kung asked if there were a single verb that you could practice thru life up to the end.

He said: Sympathy [L. reciprocity], what you don't want (done to) yourself, don't inflict on another.

XXIV

1. He said: Whom have I run down or puffed up? If I've overpraised any one he had something worth examining.

2. This people had the stuff in 'em (the timber) which

enabled the three dynasties to find the straight way and go along it (the timber whereby, the wherewithal).

XXV

1. Even I reach back to a time when historians left blanks (for what they didn't know), and when a man would lend a horse for another to ride; a forgotten era, lost.

XXVI

1. He said: Elaborate sentences, worked up words confuse the straightness of action from inwit, lack of forebearance in small things, messes up greater plans.

XXVII

1. He said: When the mob hate a man it must be examined; when everybody likes a man, it must be examined, and how!

XXVIII

1. He said: A man can put energy into the process, not the process into the man. [*Ovvero*: a man can practice the right system of conduct magnanimously, but the fact of there being a right way, won't make a man use it.]

XXIX

1. He said: To go wrong and not alter (one's course) can be defined (definitely) as going wrong.

XXX

1. He said: I've gone a whole day without eating, (*or even*: I've tried going a whole day without eating) and a whole night without sleep, meditating without profit, it's not as useful as studying particular data (grinding it up in the head).

XXXI

1. He said: The proper man plans right action, he does not scheme to get food: he can plow, and there be famine: he can study, and perhaps get a salary; the proper man is concerned with the right action, he is not concerned with the question of (his possible) poverty.

XXXII

1. He said: Intelligent enough to arrive, not man enough to hang onto; though he succeed, he will fail.

2. Intelligent enough to get a job, man enough to keep it, not go through his work soberly, folk won't respect him.

3.   Intelligent enough to get, man enough to hold, regular in his work but not following the correct procedure, no glory.

XXXIII

1.   He said: You cannot know a proper man by small things, but he can take hold of big ones, a small man cannot take hold of great things, but you can understand him by the small.

XXXIV

1.   He said: The folk's humanity is deeper than fire or water, I've seen people die from standing on fire or water. I have seen no one die from taking a stand on his manhood.

> (*Much of the raciness of Kung's remarks must lie in the click of a phrase, and the turning of different facets of the word.*)   Shen 5724, tao 6140, *if in sense of violate, one can read the remark as deep irony.*

XXXV

1.   He said: Manhood's one's own, not leavable to teacher.

> [*Tang, 6087, has very interesting complex of meanings, among which*: undertake, fill an office. *L. nearer meaning*: functioning of manhood cannot be handed over to teacher, *more ironically*: pedagogue.]

XXXVI

1.   He said: The proper man has a shell and a direction (*chen*[1]).

> *This* chen *is a key word, technical, from the "Changes" it is more than the ataraxia of stoics, the insensitivity, ability to "take it." It implies going somewhere. The Confucian will find most terms of Greek philosophy and most Greek aphorisms lacking in some essential; they have three parts of a necessary four, or four parts where five are needed, nice car, no carburetor, gearshift lacking.*

He does not merely stick to a belief [*pictogram: word and lofty, or capital*].

XXXVII

1.   He said: Serving a prince put reverence into the service, feeding comes second.

XXXVIII

1.   He said: See that education has no snob divisions.

XL

1. He said: Problem of style? Get the meaning across and then STOP.

XLI

1. Mien the (blind) musician called, when they reached the steps Confucius said: Steps; when they came to the mat, he said: Mat; when all were seated he said: So-and-so's there; so-and-so's over there.

2. Master Mien went out. Tze-chang asked: Is it correct speak to the music master in that way?

3. He said: That is correct when helping the blind.

BOOK SIXTEEN

Ke She
The Head of Chi

I

1. The head of the Chi clan was about to attack Chwan-yu.

2. Zan Yu and Chi-lu went to see Kung-tze, saying: The Chi Boss is going to give Chwan-yu the works.

3. Kung-tze said: Ain't that your fault, Hook?

4. It's a long time since one of the earlier kings appointed the headman of Chwan-yu to hold the sacrifices in East Mang, and it is in the middle of our own territory, the man who officiates at its chthonian and grain rites is one of our state servants, how can one attack it?

5. Zan Yu said: Our big man wants to, we two ministers are both against it.

6. Kung-tze said: Hook, Chau Zan used to say: While using your power, keep line; when you cannot, retire. How can one serve as guide to a blind man, if he do not support him, or help him up when he falls?

7. Moreover, your words err, when a tiger or rhino [P. *buffle*] gets out of its stockade, when a turtle or jewel is broken in its casket, whose fault is that?

8. Zan Yu said: But Chwan-yu is now strong, and near Pi, if he don't take it now it will make trouble for his sons and grandsons in coming generations.

9. Kung-tze said: Hook, you make a proper man sick refus-

ing to say: I want, and needing to make a discourse about it.

10. Me, Hillock. I have heard that men who have states or head families are not worried about fewness, but worried about fairness [*potter's wheel ideogram: aliter as verb*: worried about ruling justly], not worried about scarcity, but worried about disquiet. If every man keeps to his own land, there will be no poverty, with harmony there will be no lack of population but tranquillity without upsets (subversions).

11. It's just like that. Therefore if distant people do not conform, one should attract them by one's own disciplined culture, and by honest action, when they have come in, they will quiet down.

12. You, Yu and Ch'iu, are now aides to your big man, distant tribes do not come in, and cannot come [L. he cannot attract them]. The state is divided and decadent, people are going away and splitting up, the state can't hold onto them [L. he cannot preserve it].

13. And he plans to take up shield and lance inside the territory. I am afraid the Chi grandsons' trouble is not in Chwan-yu, it is inside their own door-yard, behind their own gate-screen. [Hsiao[1], troublesome, *or even* whistling round their gate-screen. M. *gives* ch'iang, *merely as* wall. 2620.]

II

1. Kung-tze said: When the empire is decently governed, the rites, music (musical taste), police work and punitive expeditions proceed from the Child of Heaven; when the empire is not governed, these proceed from the feudal chiefs. When they are decided by these princes, they usually lose (sovereignty) within ten generations. When these (rites, etc.) proceed from the great officers the loss usually occurs within five generations; when the subsidiary ministers in charge of the states give the orders, they usually smash within three generations.

2. When the empire is properly governed the government is NOT in the control of the great officers.

3. When the empire is properly governed, the folk don't discuss it.

III

1. Kung-tze said: For five generations the revenue has not come in to the ducal house. The government was seized by the

great officers, four generations ago, the three lines of the Hwan (Dukes) are mere epigones.

IV

1. Kung-tze said: There are three valuable friendships, and three harmful. Friendship with the straight, with the faithful [Liang, 3947 b. *not in sense as above in* XV, xxxvi, *has also sense:* considerate] and with the well-informed are an augment; making a convenience of snobs, nice softies (excellent squshies), and of pliant flatterers does one harm.

V

1. Kung-tze said: There are three pleasures which augment a man, three that harm. The pleasure of dissociating perceptions of rites and music; pleasure in other men's excellence; the pleasure in having a lot of friends with talent and character, augment; the enjoyment of swank, loafing and debauchery, harm.

VI

1. Kung-tze said: When you manage to meet a proper man, there are three committable errors: to speak when it is not up to you to speak, *videlicet* hastiness; not to speak when you should, that's called covertness; and to speak without noting a man's expression, that is called blindness.

VII

1. Kung-tze said: The proper man guards against three things; in youth before the blood and spirits have come to orderly course, he guards against taking root in luxurious appearances; at maturity when the blood and spirits are in hardy vigour, he guards against quarrelsomeness; and in old age when the blood and spirits have waned, against avarice.

VIII

1. Kung-tze said: The proper man has three awes; he stands in awe of the decrees of destiny [*heaven's mouth and seal*], he stands in awe of great men, and of the words of the sages.
2. The piker does not recognize the decrees of heaven, he is cheeky with great men, and sneers at the words of the sages.

IX

1. Kung-tze said: Those who know instinctively (as at birth) are the highest; those who study and find out, come next; those who are hampered and study come next [k'un, *hampered, a tree boxed in, limited, in poverty, chance of growth. In dis-*

tress, weary]. Those who are boxed in [L. stupid] and do not study constitute the lowest people.

X

1. Kung-tze said: The proper man has three subjects of meditation; in seeing, that he see with intelligence [*or* with his intelligence, *definite pictogram of moving eye and light from above, very strong and very inclusive phrase*], in hearing, that he hear accurately, i.e. apprehend [*the component mind in lower rt/ of ideogram, get the meaning*], that his appearance be serene, his bearing respectful, and that his speech come from the plumb centre of his mind (not slanty), that his affairs maintain reverence [*I do not think this ideogram can be too far separated from the original source, it has to do with vegetative order*]; when in doubt, that he ask questions, and when enraged that he think of troublesome consequence; when he sees the chance of gain, that he think of equity.

Up to now we have had many definitions of words, several chapters define or dissociate categories, ref/ Ta S'eu, *testament, verses* 3,4.

XI

1. Kung-tze said: Seeing the good as if unreachable; seeing evil as if it were boiling to the touch; I have seen such men, and heard such talk.

2. Living in retirement to find out what they really want, practicing equity to carry into conduct. I have heard conversation about this, but have not seen such men.

XII

1. Duke Ching of Ch'i had a thousand quadriga, on the day of his death (even at his funeral) the people did not praise his honesty [L. not praise for single virtue]. Po-i and Shu-ch'i died of hunger 'neath Southslope Head and the folk praise them down to this day.

2. That illustrates what I was saying.

Kung-fu-tzu's son

XIII

1. Ch'an K'ang asked Po-yu if he had heard anything "different" [i.e. *from what K. told the rest of them*].

2. He replied: No, he was standing alone (one day) **as I was**

passing the hall in a hurry (or going by the court-yard), he said: Studied the odes? (*Or* are you studying the odes?)

I replied: No.

"Not study the odes, won't be able to use words."

I went out and studied the Odes.

3.   Another day he was again standing alone, I went by the court in a hurry.   Said: Studying the rites?

Replied: No.

"If you don't study the rites you won't be able to stand up" (build up a character).

I went out and studied the Rites.

4.   Those are the two things I've heard (from him).

5.   Ch'an K'ang retired saying delightedly: Asked one question and got to three things.   I heard of the Odes, I heard of the Book of Rites, I heard that a proper man don't nag his son.

XIV

1.   The wife of the prince of a state is styled by the prince: The distinguished person; she calls herself: Small child; the people of the state call her: The Prince's distinguished person; those of other states style her: Little small sovran, and of (still) other states style her Prince's distinguished person.

BOOK SEVENTEEN

Yang Ho
(a minister who had usurped power)

I

1.   Yang Ho wanted to see Confucius (Kung-tze), Kung-tze did not see him.   He sent Kung-tze a pig.   Kung-tze, timing to miss him, went out to pay his duty call, but met Yang on the road.

2.   He said: I want to talk to you: keeping treasure inside you, country in chaos, call that manly?

Said: No.

"In love with work (in love with following the service) continually missing the time, call that intelligent?"

Said: No.

"Sun and moon move, the year don't wait for you."

Said: O. K.   I'll take office.

II

He said: Men are born pretty much alike, it's practising something that puts the distance between them.

III

He said: Only those of highest intelligence, and lowest simplicity do not shift. [L. cannot be changed, *text probably includes both meanings.*]

IV
(*On cultural persuasion*)

1. At Battle-Wall he heard the sound of stringed instruments and singing.

2. The big man smiled with pleasure saying: Why use an ox knife to kill a fowl?

3. Tze-yu replied, I'm the man, sir, who once heard you say: If the gentleman studies the process and loves men, the lower people will study the process and be easy to rule. [*I suppose Yen Tze-yu was in charge of this frontier town on a crag.*]

4. He said: You fellows, Yen's words are on the line, I was just joking round it.

V

1. Kung-shan Fu-zao giving trouble in the passes [field paths, 4896, short-cuts, *hence vb/* rebel] of Pi, invited him and he (Confucius) wanted to go.

2. Tze-lu was "not amused," said: Not to be done, that's that. Why must you poke into that Kung-shan gang?

3. He said: The man's invited me, suppose I go with him [*aliter:* is that empty, an empty gesture. *Depends on which sense one gives to 6536 (or c)* t'u], suppose he should make use of me, couldn't I create a Chou in the East?

VI

Tze-chang asked Kung-tze about manhood. Kung-tze said: To be able [neng², *power in union, as differing from k'e, power to support, hold up, carry*] to practice five things (all together) would humanize the whole empire.

(Chang) asked clarification.

Said: Sobriety (? *serenitas*), magnanimity, sticking by one's word, promptitude (in attention to detail), kindliness (*caritas*).

Serenity will shape things so that you will not be insulted.

274

With magnanimity you will reach the mass.

Keep your word and others will confide [*also:* trust you enough to employ you].

By promptitude you will get thru your jobs (meritorious work).

Kindliness is enough to get results from those you employ.

VII

1. Pi Hsi invited him and he wanted to go.

Tze-Lu said: I, Sprout, am the chap who heard you say, sir, "When a man personally does evil, a proper man won't enter [won't go into (it with him)]．

Pi-Hsi is in rebellion in Chung-mau. If you go, what's that like?

2. He said: I said it. But isn't it said: You can grind a hard thing without making it thin.

Isn't it said: Some white things can be dipped and not blackened. [*Cf. G. Guinicelli*].

3. Am I like a bitter melon, to be hung up and not eaten?

VIII

1. He said: Sprout, have you heard the six terms (technical terms) and the six befuddlements (overgrowings)?

Replied: No.

2. "Sit down, I'll explain 'em to you."

3. Love of manhood minus love of study: befuddlement into naïveté.

Love of knowledge without love of study: runs wild into waste incorrelation.

Love of keeping one's word, without study runs amok into doing harm.

Love of going straight without studying where to, degenerates into bad manners.

Love of boldness without love of study, leads to chaos.

Love of hard edge (hardness, stiffness) leads to impertinence.

IX

1. He said: Mes enfants, why does no one study the great Odes? [*Or more probably:* these Odes.]

2. The Odes can exhilarate (lift the will).

3. Can give awareness (sharpen the vision, help you spot the bird).

4. Can teach dissociation. [*L. takes it as:* exchange, sociability.]

5. Can cause resentment (against evil).

L. regulate feelings ?? katharsis ?? means of dealing with resentment. I mistrust a soft interpretation.

6. Bring you near to being useful to your father and mother, and go on to serving your sovran.

7. Remember the names of many birds, animals, plants and trees.

X

He said to (his son) Po-Yu: You go to work on the Chao-South and Shao-South poems. A man who hasn't worked on the Chao-nan and Shao-nan is like one who stands with his face to a wall.

XI

He said: Rites, they say, Rites! How do we place the jewels and the silk robes? Music, they say, Music! Where do the gongs and drums stand? [*Mind on instruments not on shape of the music.*]

XII

He said: Hard as a whetstone outside and wobbly as grass (or squshy) inside is rather like a picayune fellow who bores a hole in a wall to steal.

XIII   2556

He said: These (? lenient) village prototypes are purloiners (con men) acting on a conscience not their own [*L. takes* yuan² (7725) *as equiv.;* 7727. *? Rousseauequers*] good careful, thieves of virtue. [*P: cherchent les suffrages des villageois. Note* 7725 a.]

XIV

He said: To pass on wayside gossip and smear with scolding is to defoliate one's candour.

T'u² is primarily smear, secondarily road, with binome L. and M. tell what one has heard on the road.

General sense perfectly clear, the verse is against careless gossip and ill-natured slander, "smear-scold" is there in the pictogram if one wants it.

(To waste acts proceeding from clear conscience) is to stop acting on one's own inner perceptions.

XV

1. He said: How can one serve a prince along with these village-sized (kinky) minds?

2. Until they get on they worry about nothing else, and, when they have, they worry about losing the advantages.

3. When they are afraid of losing (advantages, privileges) there is nothing, absolutely nothing they will not do to retain (them) (no length they won't go to).

XVI

1. He said: Men of old had three troubles which no longer exist.

2. The old uppishness was reckless (ostentatious), the present uppishness, mere dissipation;

> [*Might say,* old was hearty, present dissolute. Excess vs. pettiness, petty leaks. Exuberance vs. license. *There is nothing in such brief statements unless they are taken as fixing the meaning and usage of the words.*]

the old punctilio [attention, *cd. almost be point of honour*] was modest (implying consideration of values), the present is mere peevishness; the old simplicity was direct, the present consists in thinking you can fool others by simple wheezes, [*or simply:* is faked] and that's that.

XVII

He said: Elaborate phrases and a pious expression (L.M. insinuating) seldom indicate manliness.

XVIII

He said: I hate the way purple spoils vermilion, I hate the way the Chang sonority confuses the music of the Elegantiae, I hate sharp mouths (the clever yawp, mouths set on profits) that overturn states and families.

XIX

1. He said: I'd like to do without words.

2. Tze-kung said: But, boss, if you don't say it, how can we little guys pass it on?

3. He said: Sky, how does that talk? The four seasons go on, everything gets born. Sky, what words does the sky use?

XX

Zu Pei wanted to see Kung-tze. Kung-tze declined on account of illness. As the messenger was going out the front door, he took his lute and sang so that the latter could hear.

L. notes indicate that Zu had probably asked advice before and not taken it, and that the call was fake, try on.

XXI

1. Tsai Wo asked about three years' mourning, wasn't one full year enough?

2. He said: If gentlemen do not observe the rites, the rites will go to ruin; if music is not played for three years the music will slip down.

3. The old (good) grain is exhausted, the new grain has risen; fire you kindle by twirling wood is a different fire, you can stop at the end of a year.

L. put in idea that "kindling by friction we go thru all the changes of wood" on the belief that they used different kinds of wood drills at different seasons, elm, willow, in spring, date, almond in summer. I should be more inclined to think that Kung indicates a break in continuity, but ends on the note: but do it if you like. Cf. verse 6 below.

4. He said: You'd feel at ease eating your rice and wearing embroidered clothes?

Said: Quite.

5. He said: If you can feel easy, go ahead, but the proper man during the period of mourning does not savour sweet food, does not delight in hearing music, does not feel easy in cushy surroundings, and therefore does not indulge, but if you now feel easy about it, go ahead.

6. Tsai Wo went out.

He said: He is not fully humane, a child does not leave its parental arms till it is three; three years' mourning is observed everywhere under heaven, did (Tsai Wo) Yu have three years' parental affection?

I suggest that the mediaeval debate between active and contemplative life is moderated in the old Chinese disposition, the need of contemplative period being answered by the years of mourning.

XXII

He said: Stuffing in food all day, nothing that he puts his mind on, a hard case! Don't chess players at least do something and have solid merit by comparison?

XXIII

Tze-lu said: Does the proper man honour bravery?

He said: The proper man puts equity at the top, if a gentleman have courage without equity it will make a mess; if a mean man have courage without equity he will steal.

XXIV

1. Tze-kung said: Does the proper man have his hatreds also?

Said: He has hates, he hates those who proclaim the ill doing of others; he hates those who live below the current and slander those above; he hates those who are bold without observing the rites (don't use their courage rightly, audacious in outraging the proper procedures), he hates those who obstinately presume and obstruct* [or, who are satisfied to presume and obstruct.]

2. Said: Granty, have you any hates?

"Hate those who snoop and pretend they have found out by intelligence; hate those who think brashness is courage; hate blabbers who pretend they do it from honesty."

XXV

He said: Young women and small men [L. *in sense of: flappers and house boys*] are hard to rear, familiarity loses respect, and aloofness rouses resentment.

XXVI

He said: If a man is hateful at forty he'll be so to the end.

BOOK EIGHTEEN

Wei Tze
The Viscount of Wei

I

(*Decline of the Yin Dynasty*)

1. The Viscount of Wei retired. The Viscount of Chi became a slave. Pi-kan protested and died.

2. Kung-tze said: Yin had three men (with a capital M).

II

1. Hui of Liu-Hsia, chief criminal judge, was dismissed three

---

* P. v. interesting and probably right *"qui s'arrêtent,"* plus the explanation (*au milieu de leurs entreprises sans avoir le cœur de les achever*), i.e. stop halfway because they haven't the guts to finish.

times. Someone said: Isn't it about time for you to clear out?

Said: Going straight and being useful to others, where would I go and not be fired three times? If I want to go crooked, what need of leaving my parental country?

III

1. Duke Ching of Ch'i awaiting Kung-tze said: I can't treat him a Chi chief, but something between that and a Mang chief.

Said: I am an old man, I can't make use of his theories (can't use the Confucian procedure). [*Thus L. but hard to get from text strictly more than* cannot use. Employ him, give him office.] Kung-tze proceeded, traveled [L. took departure].

IV

1. Ch'i folk (? the man of Ch'i) sent a present of female musicians (corps de ballet), Chi Hwan accepted them and did not hold court for three days. Confucius traveled.

V

1. The madman of Ch'u, Chieh-yu, passed Kung-tze, singing out: "Phoenix, oh Phoenix, how is your clarity fallen, no use blaming what's past, you might look out for what's to come. There's danger to anyone who goes into this present government."

2. Confucius got down (from his carriage) and wanted to talk with him but (Chieh) hurried away, so he could not.

VI

1. Ch'ang-tsu and Chieh-ni were teamed plowing [*Plowmen worked in pairs* / vide Odes etc.]. Kung-tze going by, sent Tze-lu to ask about the ford.

2. Ch'ang-tsu said: Who's that driving?

Tze-lu said: Kung Hillock.

Said: Kung Hillock of Lu?

Said: Yes.

Said: He knows the ford.

3. (Tze-lu then) asked Chieh-ni.

Chieh-ni said: Who are you, sir?

Said: I'm Sprout, secundus.

Said: A pupil of Kung Hillock of Lu?

Replied: Yes . . .

Said: "Disorder overfloods all the empire, who has the means to change it? Moreover, rather than follow a man who leaves one chief after another, better follow a scholar who has given up the world (this generation) altogether." He did not stop covering up the seed in his furrow.

4. Tze-lu went and reported, the big man sighed: One cannot collaborate with birds and beasts. If I don't work with these people whom can I work with? If the empire were on the right track, it would not need me, Hillock, to change it. [*Or* I would not give (myself, or effort) to change it.]

VII

1. Tze-lu was lagging behind and met an old man carrying a basket of weeds, on a staff over his shoulder. Tze-lu asked: Have you seen my big man?

The old man said: See by your arms and legs you haven't done any work; don't know the five grains one from another, who is your big man? He put down his stave and started weeding.

2. Tze-lu bowed and stood before him.

3. He kept Tze-lu for the night, killed a chicken, fixed the millet and fed him, introduced his two sons.

4. At sun-up Tze-lu went on and told of this.

He said: A recluse; sent Tze-lu back to see him again. When he arrived, the old man was gone.

5. Tze-lu said: It's not right not to take office.

You can't neglect the relations between old and young, how can he neglect the right relation between prince and minister, wishing to conserve his personal purity, he lets loose chaos in the great order. A proper man takes a government job, goes straight. He knows perfectly well perfect principles are not followed [*or* he knows in the end that they aren't (universally) followed].

VIII

1. The men who have retired: Po-i, Shu-ch'i, Yu-chung, I-yi, Chu-chang, Hui of Liu-hsia, Shao-lien.

2. He said: Not lowering their aims, not disgracing themselves, Po-i, Shu-ch'i. I'd say.

3. Can say Hui of Liu-hsia, and Shao-lien did lower their aims, did undergo personal shame, but their words were centred in reason and their acts worth consideration. That's all.

4. Can say of Yu-chung and I-yi, they went to live in retirement and talked. They kept themselves pure [M:], in their retirement they hit the mean of opportunism (wasted in midbalance).

5. I differ from these models, I have no categoric can and cannot.

IX

(Dispersion of the musicians of Lu)

1. The grand music master Chih went to Ch'i.

2. Kan, conductor for second meal, went to Ch'u.

Liao, "third meal," went to Ts'ai.

Chueh, "fourth meal," went to Ch'in.

3. The drummer Fang Shu went into the Honan [L. north of the river].

4. Wu, the hand drum, went to Han.

5. Yang the assistant conductor, and Hsiang the musical stone went to the sea.

X

1. The Duke of Chau said to the Duke of Lu, a proper man does not neglect his relatives; he does not grieve his great ministers by keeping them useless; he does not cast off the old without great reason. [L. members of old families?]

XI

1. Chau had eight officers; Po-ta; Po-kwo, Chung-tu, Chung-hwu, Shu-ya, Shu-hsia, Chi-sui, Chi-kwa.

BOOK NINETEEN

Tze-Chang

I

1. Tze-Chang said: The scholar-gentleman* sees danger and goes thru to his fate [L. sacrifice life]; when he sees a chance of getting on he thinks of equity, at sacrifices his thoughts are full of reverence for the powers of vegetation; in mourning, of grief; that is perhaps a complete definition.

II

1. Tze-Chang said: To comprehend acting straight from the conscience, and not put energy into doing it, to stick to the letter of the right process and not be strong in it, can you be doing with that sort? Does it matter what becomes of them? To believe in the right course, and not maintain it.

---

* The *shih* might very well have been translated knight in the age of European chivalry on various counts.

III

1. Tze-hsia's pupils asked Tze-Chang about friendly association.

Tze-Chang said: What does Tze-hsia say?

Replied: Tze-hsia says share it with those who can and ward off those who cannot. [*L. adds "advantage you."* The chiao¹ *covers the meanings:* pay, exchange, communicate. *Say:* with whom there can be an exchange.]

Tze-chang said: Differs from what I've heard, i.e. the proper man honours solid merit and is easy on the multitude, praises the honest and pities the incompetent. If I have enough solid talent what is there in men I can't put up with? If I haven't solid merit men will be ready enough to ward me off, why should I ward off others?

IV

1. Tze-hsia said: If a mean contrivance functions there must be something in it worth attention, but carry it far: 'ware mud. That's why the proper man doesn't use it.

V

1. Tze-hsia said: To be daily aware of what he lacks, not forgetting what he can make function (capacity due to what bits of knowledge he has put together), can be defined as loving study.

VI

1. Tze-hsia said: Extending study, keeping the will hard yet supple; putting a fine edge on one's questions, and stickin' close to what one really thinks. Manhood takes root in the centre of these.

VII

1. Tze-hsia said: Artificers (the hundred works) live in a market amid the outlay of their tools to perfect their technique. [*The* szu⁴ (? cf *Arab.* suk), *tools spread for use, also concurrence of shops of similar ware.*] The proper man studies so that he arrive at proceeding in the process. [*Very much:* pour savoir vivre. *Really learn how to live, up to the hilt.*]

VIII

1. Tze-hsia said: The mean man just has to gloss his faults.

IX

1. Tze-hsia said: The proper man undergoes three transfor-

mations, at a distance: stern; gentle to approach; his words firm as a grindstone.

X

1. Tze-hsia said: A proper man keeping his word [or: whose word is believed] can make the people work hard; if he don't keep his word they will consider the same work an oppression. A man who keeps his word can remonstrate with his prince, if he do not keep it, the remonstrance will be taken for insult.

XI

1. Tze-hsia said: If a man does not transgress the barriers of the great virtues, he can have leeway in small (go out and in).

XII

1. Tze-Yu said: Tze-hsia's door-men and little chaps are correct in sprinkling and sweeping, answer politely, make their entries and exits, all in a model manner, these are branches, without the root, what about it?

2. Tze-hsia heard it and said: Too bad, Tze-Yu is wrong. What does a proper man's method put first and teach and put second and loaf over? By analogy with plants and trees he divides (activities) into kinds, but how could the proper man's behaviour bring false accusation against any of them? Only the sage starts out knowing all the consequences.

XIII

1. Tze-hsia said: When the man in office has an abundance (of energy) he studies; when the studious man has an abundance he goes into office.

XIV

1. Tze-yu said: Lamentation ought to stop at the end of the mourning period.

XV

1. Tze-yu said: My friend Chang can do difficult things, oh yes, but he is not completely humane.

XVI

1. Master Tsang said: Magnificent! Chang is mag-nificent, but hard to be human with him [or: difficult to combine all that splendour with being really human].

XVII

1. Master Tsang said: I've heard our big man say you can't

tell all there is in a man until he is mourning his relatives.

XVIII

1. Master Tsang said: I've heard our big man say Mang Chwang was a true son, others can be that, but when it comes to his not changing his father's ministers, nor his father's mode of government, that is hard for 'em to match.

XIX

1. The Mang chief having made him chief criminal judge, Yang Fu questioned Master Tsang. Master Tsang said: The high-ups have lost the way, the people have been in disorder for a long time, when you find it out, pity 'em, don't think yourself clever.

"A bad name"

XX

1. Tze-kung said: "Crupper's" uncleanness wasn't as low as all that. That's why the proper man hates living at the bottom of the drain-slope where all the rot flows down.

XXI

1. Tze-kung said: A superior man's errors are like solar and lunar eclipses, when he goes wrong everyone sees it, when he comes back to course again all lift their faces. [Yang *can also mean*: trust.]

XXII

1. Kung-sun Ch'ao of Wei asked Tze-kung: How did Chung-ni (Chung secundus, Confucius) study?

2. Tze-kung said: Wan and Wu's system hadn't completely collapsed, the men of solid talent conserved the great features (the great parts of it were rooted in their memory) and the minor items were rooted in the memories of the men without talents, no one was wholly without something of Wan and Wu's method, how could the big man help studying it, though without an ordinary teacher?

XXIII

1. Shu-sun Wu-shu said to a high court officer: Tze-kung is superior to Chung-ni.

2. Tze-fu Ching-po told Tze-kung, Tze-kung said: By analogy with a house wall, mine is shoulder high, one can look over it at the house and family, and what is good in them.

3. The big man's wall is many times the height of an eight-footer, if you don't find the door and go in, you can't see the

splendour of the feudal temple, or the hundred officers' riches.

4. But how few find the door, wasn't that big chap's remark perfectly suited to him?

XXIV

1. Shu-san Wu-shu spoke ill of Chung-ni. Tze-kung said: It's no use, you can't break him down. It's the other men that are "hillocks" [*play on Confucius' familiar name Ch'iu "hillock"*] and hummocks that one can walk up. Chung-ni, the sun, the moon you cannot walk up stairs to. Though a man wants to cut himself off what harm does that do to the sun and moon, many people see them who cannot measure a meridian. [*The pictogram is a measure of the sun-rise, rather than of capacity, as L.*]

XXV

1. Ch'an Tze-ch'in said to Tze-kung, You are overdoing this respectfulness, how is Chung-ni more talented than you are?

2. Tze-kung said: The proper man can be known from a single sentence and one sentence is enough to show what a man does not know. Can't neglect keeping the word aligned with the mind.

3. You can't reach the big man, just as you can't get to heaven by walking up stairs.

4. If the big man were in charge of a state or clan, what is properly called establishment would be established, the proper system would work, the traces would be hitched so that they would draw, energies would be harmonized. He would be splendid in life, lamented in death, how can one match him?

BOOK TWENTY

I

1. Yao said: Attent! you Shun, heaven's calendar [*sun under grain under cover*] has now pulsed through in its count to take root in your personal strength, hang onto what it is all about, hand and foot (biceps and legs) if within the four seas there be dearth and exhaustion, the defining light of heaven [L. heaven's revenue] will come to perpetual end.

2. Shun gave the same sealed order to Yü. [T'ang, *as in the* Shu IV, iii, 3.]

3. Said: I, the little child Li ("Shoe") dare to use the black victim; dare clearly announce to the Whiteness above all White-

286

ness above all kings, to the Dynasty Overspreading; dare not pardon offences, nor let those who serve the spread cloth of heaven be overgrown; their report roots in the mind of the O'erspreading.

If in us, the emperor's person, be fault, it is not by the myriad regions, if the myriad regions have fault, it takes root from our person. [*Cf.* Wu, *in the* Shu V. iii.]

4. Chao had a great conferring: honest men could be rich.

5. Although he had the Chao relatives, not a matter of someone else's manhood, if the hundred clans err, it is rooted in me the one man.

6. He kept watch over the balances (weights) and the measuring [*I shd/ say* taking the sun. L./ measures], he investigated the statutes and regulations [*or better:* the functioning of the regulations, how they worked, whether they worked. *La Vie du Droit*], he combed out the useless officials, and the government of the Four Coigns went ahead.

7. He built up wasted states, restored broken successions, promoted men who had retired, and the people of the empire returned to good sense.

8. What he put weight on was feeding the people, mourning and offerings.

9. By magnanimity reached to everyone; by keeping his word got their trust; got thru a lot of work by attention to detail and kept them happy by justice.

II

1. Tze-chang asked Kung-tze how one should carry on government.

He said: Honour the five excellences and throw out the four evils.

Tze-chang said: How do you define the five excellences?

He said: The proper man [*here,* man-in-authority] is considerate without being extravagant, energetic (or even urging) without grumbling, desires without greed, is honourable without hauteur, and boldly protective without ferocity.

2. Tze-chang said: What do you mean by being considerate not extravagant? He said: Cause the people to profit by what he profits by (their cut of grain), isn't that being considerate without extravagance? When he picks out the right work for them, they work, who will grumble; desiring manhood and

attaining it, is that greed? Whether he is dealing with many or few, with small matter or great, the proper man does not venture to be churly, is not that being honourable and not haughty? The proper man adjusts his robe and cap, honours what is clearly worthy of honour, [Occhio per la mente. *If a strict stylist is distinguishing* chien (4) 860 M *and* shih (4) 5789, *the former wd/ be* eye-sight *and the latter, I take it,* mind-sight, intellectual clarity] with dignity so that others look up to him and even fear him, isn't that severity without ferocity?

3 Tze-chang said: How define the four evils? He said: Not to teach people and then put them to death is cruelty; not to warn people and then expect them to have things finished perfectly, is called oppression. [*L. admirably:* to require suddenly the full tale of work without having given warning.] To be dilatory (sloppy) in giving orders and exigent in expecting them carried out at the precise date is cheating.

6752. *This* tse (2-5) *certainly cannot be translated* thief *in all contexts, it is an abusive term, centre of meaning seems to be nearer to "cheat" though theft is certainly included. "Con game" with violence, any thieving trick.*
As in giving to others, to come out and give in a stingy manner
Thus L., but if we are getting down to brass tacks, I should think the ch'u na: go out-insert, *might refer to the familiar "kick-back," getting personal repayment from an official payment to another.*
called having assistant-officers.
Unless it refers to kick-back *or something more than manner, seems hardly great enough to be listed among the four hateful or evil things.* 4809. o(4-5). *That is to say it wd/ seem to be stretching the* o(4-5) *into a milder meaning than it usually has in the* Four Books. P. on appelle cela se comporter comme un collecteur d'impots.

III

1. He said: Not to know the decree [the sealed mouth. *L. adds "of heaven," not to recognize destiny*] is to be without the means of being a proper man (the ancestral voice incomplete).

2. Not to know the rites is to be without means to construct.

3. Not to know words (the meaning of words) is to be without the fluid needful to understand men.